HEMINGWAY'S SHORT STORIES

NOTES

including
- *Life and Background of the Author*
- *Introduction to the Stories*
- *A Brief Synopsis*
- *List of Characters*
- *Critical Commentaries*
- *Character Analyses*
- *Critical Essays*
- *CliffsNotes Review*
- *CliffsNotes Resource Center*
- *Selected Bibliography*

by
James L. Roberts, Ph.D.
University of Nebraska–Lincoln

Cliffs Notes

INCORPORATED

LINCOLN, NEBRASKA 68501

Publishing Director
Greg Tubach

Development, Project, and
Copy Editor
Sherri Fugit

Senior Production Project
Coordinator
E. Shawn Aylsworth

ISBN 0-7645-8552-5
Library of Congress Catalog Card No.:00-101156
© Copyright 2000
by
Cliffs Notes, Inc.
All Rights Reserved
Printed in the U.S.A.

2000 Printing

Cliff Notes, Inc.   Lincoln, Nebraska

CONTENTS

HEMINGWAY'S SHORT STORIES

Notes

LIFE AND BACKGROUND OF THE AUTHOR

Ernest Hemingway's colorful life as a war correspondent, big game hunter, angler, writer, and world celebrity, as well as winner of the 1954 Nobel Prize in literature, began in quiet Oak Park, Illinois, on July 21, 1899. When Ernest, the first son and second child born to Dr. Ed and Grace Hemingway, was only seven weeks old, his general practitioner father took the family for a quick weekend trip to the Michigan north woods, where Dr. Hemingway was having land cleared by several Ottawa Indians for Windemere, a summer cabin that he built on Walloon Lake. Ernest would return to this area year after year, as a child and later as an adolescent—hunting, fishing, camping, vegetable gardening, adventuring, and making plans for each new, successive summer.

Ernest's mother, a devout, religious woman with considerable musical talent, hoped that her son would develop an interest in music; she herself had once hoped for an operatic career, but during her first recital at Carnegie Hall, the lights were so intense for her defective eyes that she gave up performing. Ernest attempted playing the cello in high school, but from the beginning, it was clear that he was no musician. Instead, he deeply shared his father's fierce enthusiasm for the outdoors.

Ernest began fishing when he was three years old, and his fourth birthday present was an all-day fishing trip with his father. For his twelfth birthday, his grandfather gave him a single-barrel 20-gauge shotgun. His deep love of hunting and fishing in the north Michigan woods during his childhood and adolescence formed lasting impressions that would be ingredients for his short stories centering around Nick Adams, Hemingway's young fictional persona.

In high school, Hemingway played football, mostly lightweight football, because he was small and thin. Hoping for more success in another sport, Hemingway took up boxing. Years later, he would often write, using boxing metaphors; he would also tell people that it was a boxing accident that was responsible for his defective eyesight. Hemingway was always self-conscious about seeming less than the best at whatever he chose to do. For example, he had a lifelong difficulty pronouncing his l's; his sounded like w's. His perfectionist father always stressed that whatever Ernest did, he must "do it right." The stigma of having a slight speech defect and genetically flawed eyesight continually rankled Hemingway.

Hemingway's writing career began early. He was a reporter for *The Trapeze*, his high-school newspaper, and he published a couple of stories in the *Tabula*, the school's literary magazine. Ironically, he remained an atrocious speller throughout his life. Whenever editors would complain about his bad spelling, he'd retort, "Well, that's what *you're* hired to correct!"

After Ernest's high-school graduation, Dr. Hemingway realized that his son had no passion for further education, so he didn't encourage him to enroll in college. Neither did he encourage him to join the boys his age who were volunteering for the army and sailing to Europe to fight in World War I. Instead, Dr. Hemingway took another approach: He called the Kansas City *Star* to find out if his son could sign on as a cub reporter. He learned that an opening wouldn't be available until September, news that delighted Ernest because it meant that he could spend another summer in the north Michigan woods hunting and fishing before he began working in the adult world.

Arriving in Kansas City to work for the *Star*, young Hemingway began earning fifteen dollars a week. He was taught to write short sentences, avoid clichés, unnecessary adjectives, and construct good stories. He soon realized that a large part of Kansas City life was filled with crime and impulsive violence. It was an exciting time for the naive, eager, red-cheeked young man from the north woods who was determined to learn how to write well.

A few months passed, and despite the satisfying pace of his life and the thrill of seeing his work in print, Hemingway realized that most of the young men he knew were leaving to take part in the war in Europe. Hemingway's father was still opposed to his son's joining the army, and Hemingway himself knew that his defective eyesight would probably keep him from being accepted. However, Hemingway met Theodore Brumback, a fellow reporter with vision in only one eye at the *Star*, who suggested that Hemingway volunteer for the American Field Service as an ambulance driver. Hemingway's yearning to join the war effort was rekindled, and six months after he began his career as a newspaper reporter, he and Brumback resigned from the *Star*, said goodbye to their families, and headed to New York for their physicals. Hemingway received a B rating and was advised to get some glasses.

The letters that Hemingway wrote home to his parents while he was waiting to sail overseas were jubilant. The voyage from New York to France aboard the *Chicago*, however, was less exultant. Hemingway's second typhoid shot had left him nauseated and aching, and rough seas sent him retching to the rails several times.

At Bordeaux, France, Hemingway and Brumback boarded a train headed to Milan, Italy. Shortly after they settled in, a munitions factory exploded, and Hemingway was stunned to discover that "the dead are more women than men." After a few weeks of making routine ambulance runs and transporting dying and wounded men to hospitals, Hemingway grew impatient. Wanting to see more action, he traveled to the Austro-Italian border, where he finally had a sense of being at the wartime front.

During this time near the Austro-Italian border, Hemingway was severely wounded. An Austrian projectile exploded in the trenches and sent shrapnel ripping into his legs. Trying to carry an Italian soldier to safety, Hemingway caught a machine-gun bullet behind his kneecap and one in his foot. A few days later, he found himself on a train, returning to Milan. Later, writing about being wounded, he recalled that he felt life slipping from him. Some literary critics believe that it was this near death experience that obsessed Hemingway with a continual fear of death and a need to test his courage that lasted the rest of his life.

A few months later, the war was over and Hemingway returned to the States with a limp and a fleeting moment of celebrity. At home in Oak Park, Illinois, Hemingway immediately felt homesick for Italy. All of his friends were gone, and he received a letter from a nurse with whom he'd fallen in love while he was hospitalized. The news was not good: She had fallen in love with an Italian lieutenant. Ten years later, this nurse would become the model for the valiant Catherine Barkeley in *A Farewell to Arms*.

Returning to the north woods to find his emotional moorings, Hemingway fished, wrote some short-story sketches, and enjoyed a brief romance that would figure in "The End of Something" and "The Three-Day Blow." He also spoke to women's clubs about his wartime adventures, and one of the women in the audience, a monied Toronto matron, was so impressed with Hemingway that she hired him as a companion for her lame son.

Tutoring the boy and filling a scrapbook with writings in Canada, Hemingway then headed back to the Midwest, where he met Hadley Richardson, seven years older than he and an heiress to a small trust fund.

Hadley fell in love with Hemingway. Hemingway's ever-fretting, over-protective mother thought that Hadley was exactly what her rootless son needed; she prodded Hemingway to settle down and give up his gypsy travels and short-term, part-time jobs.

Despite his fears that marriage would destroy his way of living, Hemingway married Hadley, and they set up housekeeping, living on income from her trust fund. Soon, near-poverty depleted Hemingway's usual good nature, and friends urged him to move to Paris, where living expenses would be cheaper.

In Paris, Hemingway and Hadley lived in the Latin Quarter, a bohemian enclave of artists, poets, and writers. The *Toronto Sun* bought the articles that Hemingway submitted, as well as his political sketches, and Hemingway was pleased about the short stories he was writing. He was twenty-three years old and felt that he'd finally hit his stride as an author with a style that was authentically his own.

After covering the war between Greece and Turkey for the New York *Sun*, Hemingway returned to Paris and continued writing Nick Adams tales, including "A Way You'll Never Be." He was interrupted, though, when the Toronto *Star* insisted that he cover the Lausanne Peace Conference. While there, he urged Hadley to join him, and she did so, bringing all of his short stories, sketches, and poems in a valise that would be stolen in the Lyon train station.

Hemingway was so stunned with disbelief at the terrible loss that he immediately returned to Paris, convinced that Hadley surely hadn't packed even the carbon copies of his stories, but she had. Hemingway had lost everything that he'd written.

Ironically, American expatriate and writer Gertrude Stein had just spoken to Hemingway about loss, mentioning a garage keeper's off-hand comment: "You are all a lost generation," a casual remark, yet one that eventually would become world famous after Hemingway used it as an epigraph to his first major novel, *The Sun Also Rises* (1926). This term "lost generation" would be instantly meaningful to Hemingway's readers. It would give a name to the attitudes of the post-World War I generation of Americans, especially to the young writers of that era who believed that their loves and hopes had been shattered by the war. They had been led down a glory trail to death—not for noble patriotic ideals, but for the greedy, materialistic gains of international power groups. The high-minded sentiments of their elders were not to be trusted; only reality was truth—and reality was harsh: Life was futile, often meaningless.

After the loss of his manuscripts, Hemingway followed Stein's advice to go to Spain; she promised him that he'd find new stories there. After his sojourn in Spain, Hemingway returned to Paris and from there to Canada, where Hadley gave birth to their first child. Afterward, Hemingway returned to Paris, where he began writing "Big Two-Hearted River." From there, he went to Austria, where he wrote more Nick Adams stories, as well as "Hills Like White Elephants."

Hemingway and Hadley were divorced in 1927, and he married Pauline Pfeiffer, an Arkansas heiress, who accompanied him to Africa, traveling 300 miles by train to reach Nairobi, and onward to the Kapti Plains, the foothills of the Ngong Hills, and the Serengeti Plain. Africa would be the setting for two of Hemingway's most famous short stories—"The Short Happy Life of Francis Macomber" and "The Snows of Kilimanjaro."

In 1940, Hemingway and Pauline were divorced, and he married writer Martha Gellhorn. They toured China, then established a residence in Cuba. When World War II began, Hemingway volunteered his services and his fishing boat, the *Pilar*, and cooperated with United States naval intelligence as a German submarine spotter in the Caribbean.

Wanting a still-more-active role in the war, Hemingway soon was a 45-year-old war correspondent barnstorming through Europe with the Allied invasion troops—and sometimes ahead of them. It is said that Hemingway liberated the Ritz Hotel in Paris and that when the Allied troops arrived, they were greeted by a notice on the entrance: "Papa Hemingway took good hotel. Plenty stuff in the cellar."

Following yet another divorce, this one in 1944, Hemingway married Mary Welsh, a *Time* magazine correspondent. The couple lived in Venice for a while, then returned to Havana, Cuba. In 1950, *Across the River and into the Trees* appeared, but it was neither a critical nor a popular success. His short novel *The Old Man and the Sea* (1952), however, restored Hemingway's literary stature, and he was awarded the 1953 Pulitzer Prize in literature.

In January 1954, Hemingway was off for another of his many African safaris and was reported dead after two airplane crashes in two days. He survived, though, despite severe internal and spinal injuries and a concussion. When he read newspaper obituary notices about his death, he noted with great pleasure that they were favorable. That same year, Hemingway received the Swedish Academy's Nobel Prize in literature, "for his powerful style forming mastery of the art of modern narration, as most recently evidenced in *The Old Man and the Sea.*"

During the next few years, Hemingway was not happy, and during 1961, he was periodically plagued by high blood pressure and clinical depression. He received shock therapy during two long confinements at the Mayo Clinic in Rochester, Minnesota, but most of the prescribed treatment for his depression was of little value. Hemingway died July 2, 1961, at his home, the result of a self-inflicted gunshot wound.

It seems as if there were always two Hemingways. One was the adventurer—the grinning, bearded "Papa" of the news photographs; the other was the skillful, sensitive author Hemingway, who patiently wrote, rewrote, and edited his work.

Certainly each of the short stories discussed in this volume represents a finished, polished "gem"—Hemingway's own word for his short stories. No word is superfluous, and no more words are needed. Along with such well-known short-story writers as William Faulkner, Flannery O'Connor, and John Steinbeck, Hemingway is considered by literary critics to be one of the world's finest.

INTRODUCTION TO THE SHORT STORIES

The selection of stories in this volume is based on the stories found in high-school and college literature anthologies that ranked them as not only the best of Hemingway's short story output but also as the ones taught most frequently in high-school and college American Literature courses, as well as in Introduction to Literature courses.

The importance of including Hemingway in American Literature anthologies cannot be overestimated. Hemingway's style and subject matter are archetypal of American writing. Hemingway broke new literary ground when he began publishing his short stories. Furthermore, not only was he an American writer, but he was not an ivory-tower esthete; he was a man's man. He hunted in grand style, deep-sea fished, covered both World War I and World War II for national news services, and was married as many times as Hollywood celebrities—and yet he found time to write novels and stories that feature men and women facing both death and emotional crises with grit, gumption, and grand tenacity.

Hemingway's heroes are characterized by their unflinching integrity. They do not compromise. They are vulnerable but are not defined by their vulnerability. Hemingway's men and women are often defiant of what society expects of them: They eat with gusto, devour adventure, and have sex—simply and directly.

In the beginning, Hemingway wrote about himself, and he would continue to write himself into all, or most, of his characters until his death. His first persona was Nick Adams, a young boy who accompanies a doctor to an American Indian camp and watches the doctor use a jackknife to slice into a woman's abdomen and deliver a baby boy.

At that early age, Nick vows never to die. Later, he defies death and the sanity-threatening wounds that he receives in Italy during World War I. He rotely repeats, in blind faith, the knee-bending exercises for his stiff, battle-scarred knee. Instinctively, he returns to the north woods of Michigan to heal his soul of the trauma of war. Hemingway himself suffered a bad knee wound during the war and returned to hunting and fishing in Michigan's northern woods.

In his more mature stories, such as "The Snows of Kilimanjaro" and "The Short Happy Life of Francis Macomber," Hemingway creates far more complex characters and situations for his characters. "Snows" is a stylistic tour de force, a perfect dovetailing of intense, invigorating, interior-monologue flashbacks as contrasts to sections of present-time narratives, during which the main character, a writer named Harry, is slowly dying of gangrene. Symbolically, Harry is also rotting away because of the poisonous nature of his wife's money. As his life ebbs away, he realizes that his writing talent has been ebbing away for years, as surely as his life is, symbolized by the hyena and the buzzards who wait to feast on his carcass.

"A Clean, Well-Lighted Place" and "Hills Like White Elephants" are examples of Hemingway's most pared-down style, in which he removes himself from the role of narrator. The stories are almost wholly composed of dialogue. One must engage him or herself in the narratives and ignite his or her imagination to understand the emotional core of each of these stories. Hemingway expects us to.

Hemingway's genius as an American original was evident long before he produced his novels that are today considered masterpieces of American literature. Both critics and readers have hailed his short stories as proof that a pure, true American literature was finally possible. American literature was no longer merely watered-down British reading fare. American literature had at last come into its own. Hemingway set the standard—and the writers who came after him honored his achievement.

THE NICK ADAMS STORIES

LIST OF CHARACTERS

"INDIAN CAMP"

Dr. Adams

A general practitioner and emergency surgeon who lives near a lake on the northern peninsula of Michigan. Using makeshift surgical instruments, he delivers a baby boy to an American Indian woman who has been in excruciating labor for two days.

Uncle George

Dr. Adams' brother; he accompanies Dr. Adams to the camp and with the help of three American Indian men, holds the American Indian woman down while Dr. Adams performs a cesarean.

Nick

Dr. Adams' son, about eight or nine years old; he goes with his father and uncle to the American Indian camp.

American Indian Woman

Having screamed for two days while trying to give birth, she is helped by Dr. Adams, who makes an incision in her with a jackknife and delivers a boy.

American Indian Husband

The presumed father of the baby that Dr. Adams delivers by cesarean surgery is found dead in his bed. Hearing his wife scream for two days and during the painful, crude surgery drives him mad. Silently and secretly, he cuts his throat.

"THE DOCTOR AND THE DOCTOR'S WIFE"

Dr. Henry Adams

A proud doctor who is ashamed and angry that he is teased by American Indians hired to cut up logs that broke loose from a White and McNally shipment to a sawmill downstream.

Mrs. Adams

The doctor's ailing Christian Scientist wife; she nags her husband with whining platitudes and biblical admonitions.

Nick

The son of Dr. and Mrs. Adams, Nick blindly hero-worships his father.

Dick Boulton

A mixed-blood American Indian who is hired to cut logs for Dr. Adams.

Eddy Boulton

Dick's son; he carries the long crosscut saw for cutting the logs.

Billy Tabeshaw

Dick's friend; he comes along to help cut logs.

"THE END OF SOMETHING"

Nick Adams

In his late teens, Nick is living in the Michigan north woods.

Marjorie

Nick's summertime romantic interest; Marjorie is stoic and leaves after Nick breaks off their relationship.

Bill

Nick's friend; he is more instrumental in Nick's breaking up with Marjorie than Nick himself is.

"THE THREE-DAY BLOW"

Nick Adams ("Wemedge")

A young man about eighteen years old who has just broken off a relationship with Marjorie, a girl whom he has been dating.

Bill

Nick's friend; he is jealous of the time that Nick spends with Marjorie and has urged Nick to stop dating her.

"THE KILLERS"

George

The manager of a diner in Summit, Illinois.

Nick Adams

A young man about nineteen who tries to warn a boxer that is about to be shot by a couple of hired killers. When the boxer seems passively unconcerned about his own fate, Nick leaves town because he can't stand to think about a man who succumbs so easily to the threat of death.

Sam

The Black cook at the diner.

Al

One of the hired killers; he wears a black overcoat, silk muffler, gloves, and a derby hat. Al ties up Nick and Sam.

Max

The other hired killer. He too wears a too-tight black topcoat and a derby hat. According to Al, Max talks too much, revealing their plans to kill Ole Andreson.

Ole Andreson

A boxer who has probably double-crossed someone, and this someone has, in turn, hired Al and Max to kill Ole.

Mrs. Bell

The landlady who manages Hirsch's Rooming House.

"A WAY YOU'LL NEVER BE"

Nick Adams ("Nicolo")

An American soldier who fades in and out of what he calls "craziness" after he is wounded in Italy during World War I.

Italian Second Lieutenant

He is reluctant to allow Nick to talk to the captain of the Italian military unit.

Captain Paravicini

He realizes the seriousness of Nick's wound and urges him not to bicycle back in the fierce afternoon heat.

"IN ANOTHER COUNTRY"

The Doctor

He tries to convince Nick and the Major to use the therapy machines in the hospital.

The Major ("Signor Maggiore")

Once a champion fencer, his right hand is now severely withered because of an industrial accident.

Nick Adams

An American soldier who suffers a knee wound in World War I and struggles to understand the unusually stoic major's sudden outburst of emotion.

"BIG TWO-HEARTED RIVER—PARTS I & II"

Nick Adams

A young man who was wounded in World War I and has now returned to the woods of northern Michigan to fish and to heal himself of battle trauma.

OTHER WELL-KNOWN HEMINGWAY STORIES

"THE SHORT HAPPY LIFE OF FRANCIS MACOMBER"

Francis Macomber

A wealthy sportsman and versatile athlete. When he encounters his first lion, he doesn't shoot: He runs. To himself, he seems a coward, but the next day, he demonstrates his bravery but is killed at the moment of his triumph.

Margaret Macomber ("Margot")

Francis' beautiful, domineering wife. She refuses to divorce him because of his money, but he cannot divorce her because of her beauty. Margot is delighted when Francis runs from the lion; this gives her more psychological control over him.

Robert Wilson

The guide for the Macombers on this safari, he is the essence of the Hemingway code character. He does not follow the laws and rules of society; instead, he has his own code of conduct, to which he rigidly conforms.

The Beaters

African natives who beat the grass to flush wild game into the open.

Kongoni and Abdulla

The gun-bearers: natives who accompany the hunters and track down the wounded animals. When Macomber is carried triumphantly on the arms and shoulders of the cook, the personal boys, the skinner and the porters, the gun bearers do not take part because they witnessed Macomber's cowardly flight from the lion.

"HILLS LIKE WHITE ELEPHANTS"

The Man

A young American man, unmarried, who waits with a girl in a railway station in Spain.

The Girl

Referred to by the young man as "Jig," she is trying to decide whether or not to have an abortion; she slowly becomes increasingly angry as the young man minimizes her dilemma.

"A CLEAN, WELL-LIGHTED PLACE"

The Young Waiter

Impatient to close the cafe and go home to his wife, he insults the deaf old man, who, of course, can't hear him.

The Old Waiter

An old man, like the deaf old man, he lives alone and is sympathetic to the old man's drinking until he is drunk.

The Old Man

About 80 years old and deaf, the old man is drinking brandy in the very early hours of the morning in a Spanish cafe.

"THE SNOWS OF KILIMANJARO"

Harry

Once a promising writer, he sacrificed his talent for the comfort of his wife's money. Now, dying of gangrene, he realizes that he will never be able to write the great fiction that he had envisioned. He is painfully conscious of his defeat and loss.

Helen

Harry's wife; he married her because he thought he loved her; in truth, however, he married her because of her money. Helen is a loyal, loving, affectionate, and courageous woman.

Molo

The servant who tends to Harry; his main function is to pour enough liquor in Harry so that Harry can stand the pain of his wound and that of utter disappointment.

Compson

The aviator who is supposed to arrive and take Harry to a hospital.

CRITICAL COMMENTARIES
THE NICK ADAMS STORIES

"INDIAN CAMP"

Summary

One night, Dr. Adams is summoned to help an American Indian woman who has been in painful labor for two days. The doctor takes his young son, Nick, and his brother, George, to the American Indian camp on the other side of a northern Michigan lake. There, the doctor performs impromptu, improvised cesarean with a fishing knife, catgut, and no anesthetic to deliver the baby. Afterward, he discovers that the woman's husband, who was in the bunk above hers, silently cut his throat during the painful ordeal.

Commentary

This story is a good example of the "initiation story," a short story that centers around a main character who comes into contact with an idea, experience, ritual, or knowledge that he did not previously know. Hemingway wrote a number of initiation stories, or as they are sometimes referred to, "rite of passage" stories, and the main character in most of these stories is Nick Adams, a young man much like Hemingway himself.

In this story, Nick Adams is a very young boy in the Michigan north woods, accompanying his father, Dr. Adams, and his uncle George to an American Indian camp on the other side of a lake. Hemingway's own father was a doctor, who spent much time with his son in the northern woods of Michigan (most critics read this story as somewhat autobiographical). Here, a very young Nick is initiated into concepts that remained of highest importance to Hemingway throughout his writing career: life and death; suffering, pain, and endurance; and suicide.

Nick's father goes to the American Indian camp to help a young American Indian woman who has been screaming because of severe labor pains for two days, still unable to deliver her baby. When Dr. Adams arrives, she is lying in a bottom bunk; her husband, who cut his foot badly with an axe three days before, is lying in the bunk bed above her. Doctor Adams asks Nick to assist him, holding a basin of hot water while four American Indian men hold down the woman. Using his fishing jackknife as a scalpel, Dr. Adams performs a cesarean on the woman, delivers the baby boy, then sews up the woman's incision with some gut leader line from his fishing tackle. Exhilarated by the success of his impromptu, improvised surgery, Doctor Adams looks into the top bunk and discovers that the young American Indian husband, who listened to his wife screaming during her labor pains and during the cesarean, has cut his throat.

Although this very short story deals with violence and suffering, with birth and death, sexism and racism, Hemingway's emphasis is not on the shocking events themselves; instead, Hemingway shows the effect of birth and death on young Nick Adams. Nick's progression in this short story is vividly portrayed in polarities. For instance, on the way to the camp in the boat, Nick is sitting in his father's arms; on the way back, Nick sits on the opposite end of the boat. Similarly, while his father wants Nick to witness the birth (and his surgical triumph), Nick turns his head away; when the American Indian husband is discovered dead in his bed, Nick sees it, even though his father wants to protect him from it. The fact that Nick sits across from his father in the boat on the way back after this experience can indicate a pulling out from underneath his father's influence.

The young boy asks his father why the young American Indian man cut his throat and is told, "I don't know. . . . He couldn't stand things, I guess." However, there are more subtle undercurrents for the American Indian husband's suicide as well. The treatment and attitude of Dr. Adams toward the woman, who is an American Indian, are key also. When Dr. Adams tells Nick that her screaming is not important, it is at this point that the American Indian husband rolls over in his bunk toward the shanty wall, as he is found later, after slitting his own throat with a razor. While this failure to confront the events at hand indicates fear, it can also indicate the American Indian husband's resignation to the thoughtless racism of the White men who have come to help her.

Some have suggested that Uncle George is possibly the father of the child, as he seems to have a friendly relationship with the American Indians in the beginning of the story and hands out cigars to everyone after the birth. His handing out cigars to the men present could possibly be interpreted as paternity, although one could also surmise that he is simply sharing his way of celebrating the miracle of birth with the American Indians. Additionally, he stays behind in the camp after Dr. Adams and Nick leave. Following the interpretation of Uncle George being the baby's father, the husband's suicide could be seen as an inability to deal with his own shame and the cuckoldry of his wife.

Here, Dr. Adams emphasizes to Nick that although this young American Indian man committed suicide, women rarely do. Fear conquered the young American Indian man; he did not have the courage and strength to cope with it. He failed his test of manhood. During the boat trip back across the lake, while Nick and his father are talking, the reader learns that Nick feels "quite safe—that he would never die." Even at this young age, Nick vows never to succumb to fear. His resolve never to bow to fear is so great that he's ready to defy even the concept of natural, mortal life.

Throughout his entire writing career, Hemingway would write about men who *could* "stand things" and men who *couldn't* "stand things." Of vital importance to him was the concept of being able to "stand things," no matter how violent and painful the situation is. He called this strength "grace under pressure." A real, authentic man never succumbs; most of all, he does not kill himself. Ironically, both Hemingway and his father committed suicide.

In his later stories about Nick Adams, Hemingway explores how this young boy matures and how his vow never to bow to fear is central to the crisis in each story.

(Here and in the following sections, difficult words and phrases are explained.)

- **stern**   the rear part of a boat.

- **shanties**   crudely built cabins, or shacks.

- **interne**   a recent graduate of medical school undergoing hands-on, practical training.

- **peroxide**   a substance such as sodium peroxide that cleanses a wound.

- **St. Ignace**   a resort town on the southeast part of the northern peninsula of Michigan.

- **cesarean**   a surgical incision made through the abdomen and uterus to deliver a baby when vaginal delivery is dangerous to both mother and baby.

"THE DOCTOR AND THE DOCTOR'S WIFE"

Summary

Dr. Adams hires two American Indians to cut some logs that broke free from a shipment bobbing downstream toward a large sawmill company. They are glad to make some extra money and are in a good mood, good-naturedly teasing the doctor about stealing the logs. The doctor becomes furious and fires the men, then goes upstairs, where his wife lectures him with platitudes. Disgusted with his wife and himself, the doctor goes outside and accepts his young son's invitation to go where they can see some black squirrels.

Commentary

The doctor in the story's title refers to Dr. Adams, a central character in "Indian Camp." In that story, the doctor's son, Nick, was a boy, and after his father successfully delivered a baby with makeshift surgical implements. In this story, Nick is still a young boy and still idolizes his father. However, we see a far different

Dr. Adams than Nick does. To Nick, his father can do no wrong; readers observe Dr. Adams being a hypocritical coward. Dr. Adams may have performed heroically at the American Indian camp, but not here. Here, he's clearly a man who "can't stand it" when he's confronted with the truth about his unethical behavior.

Three Ojibway Indians have come to cut several beached logs that broke loose from the White and McNally log shipments that were being towed to the mill located down the lake from the Adams property. Doctor Adams plans to use the logs for wood for his fireplace. However, when Dick Boulton, one of the Ojibway Indians, jokes about the logs being stolen, Adams is angrily embarrassed and shamed by Boulton's knowing that Adams is fully aware that the logs rightly belong to White and McNally; he orders them off his property.

Dick has bested the doctor. He's proud that although he's ready to cut up the logs willingly for the doctor, he's not hypocritical enough — as the doctor is—to pretend that the logs don't belong to White and McNally. As a measure of his contempt for the doctor's hypocrisy, he exits by the back gate and leaves it open.

The doctor's wife is still in bed and cautions her husband with platitudes about self-control and the dangers of an unruly temper. She questions him about the Dick Boulton incident and expresses disbelief in her husband's lies about Boulton's alleged intention to not pay for the doctor's saving his wife from dying from pneumonia.

Discovering Nick reading a book under a tree, Dr. Adams tells his son that his mother wants to see him, but Nick, still obviously very much in awe of his father, the miracle-working doctor, dismisses his mother's request. He wants to go hiking with his father. Dr. Adams is grateful for his son's company; he is eager to escape—escape to anywhere, anywhere where there aren't men like Dick Boulton. Earlier, he spent a long time cleaning his gun; clearly, he'd like to shoot Boulton. Now, though, his temper somewhat in check, he's willing to go anywhere with Nick—even to the nebulous place where "there's black squirrels."

- **cross-cut saw**   a saw for cutting wood against the grain.

- **cant-hooks**   wooden levers with movable metal hooks near one end that are used for handling logs.

- **big log booms**   a chain of floating logs making a barrier to enclose other free-floating logs.

- **cord wood**   a pile of logs that will be used for burning in a fireplace.

- **half-breed**   a derogatory term used to refer to a person of mixed racial ancestry, especially American Indian and Caucasian.

- **a plug of tobacco**   a dense piece of chewing tobacco.

- **eye teeth**   the canine, or pointed and conical, teeth located in the upper jaw.

- **Christian Scientist**   a follower of Mary Baker Eddy (1821-1910), an American religious leader.

- **He who ruleth his spirit is greater than he that taketh a city.**   The quotation is from the Bible, Proverbs 16:31-32.

- **squaw**   an offensive term used to refer to a Native American woman or wife.

"THE END OF SOMETHING"

Summary

A teenager now, Nick Adams has been dating Marjorie, a girl who has been working during the summer at a resort on Hortons Bay. This evening, the two of them row to a beach on the bay. After a picnic supper, Nick tells Marjorie that he wants to break off their relationship; being with Marjorie, he says, is no longer fun. After she leaves, Nick feels bad about having to sever his friendship with Marjorie; however, he tells his friend Bill that the breakup wasn't too difficult.

Commentary

The setting is the north Michigan woods, familiar territory in Hemingway's early fiction. Nick Adams is now a young man, dating a girl named Marjorie. The story concerns not only the "end of something," but the end of three things: the end of the heydays of logging, the end of the mill town on Hortons Bay, and the end of a romance between Nick and Marjorie.

Hortons Bay is no longer a lively, fun place; its great saws, rollers, belts, and pulleys have been removed. What remains barely resembles the once-bustling, full-of-life mill town. There is nothing to remind a stranger what it used to be. Marjorie points out the ruin of the mill, romantically likening it to a castle. Nick doesn't comment on the romantic parallel that Marjorie points out.

The setting that Hemingway describes is proof that when Hortons Bay ended its noisy, financially booming years, the finale was indeed an end—and a time to move on—because the way of life that the town's inhabitants had taken for granted had vanished. This shocking revelation must have been momentous.

Nick's decision to end his romantic relationship with Marjorie will also be the "end of something," but, to Nick, it's not the end of something momentous. It's simply the end of a relationship that's gone stale, that's no longer fun.

The story is closely autobiographical. In the summer of 1919, 20 year-old Hemingway was dating 17 year-old Marjorie Bump, a waitress in a resort town. Marjorie often fixed picnic meals for them that they would eat beside evening campfires. When Marjorie's summer job ended after Labor Day, Hemingway began dating someone else. The fictional "Bill" in the story is no doubt based on Bill Smith, a good friend of Hemingway's who spent time with Hemingway that summer.

What's surprising about this very brief sketch is the amount of suppressed emotion. In 1919, the fictional (and the real) Marjorie would have typically been dating Nick Adams with marriage in mind. When Nick breaks off the relationship with only the weak explanation that being with Marjorie is no longer "fun," his remark is uncommonly cruel. In "The Three-Day Blow," we'll see that Nick prides himself on being articulate and learned. He is neither in "The End of Something." Marjorie's reaction is stoic; she doesn't even accept his offer to help push off her boat. She leaves him beside the campfire and paddles back across the bay alone.

Nick acknowledges to Bill that the breakup went "all right." There "wasn't any scene." Obviously, he and Bill had discussed what Nick had planned to do when he and Marjorie set out at the beginning of the story, rowing along the store, trolling for rainbow trout. The breakup was not spur-of-the-moment. Nick even initiated a quarrel to strengthen his revolve to break off the relationship with Marjorie.

Afterward, Nick feels bad about having to sever the friendship, but clearly, he is not looking for someone to take care of him, someone to be a domestic anchor. He has done what he had to: He has followed his instincts and made sure that he would be free to explore the world in search of fun and adventure.

- **trolling**   fishing by trailing a baited line from behind a slow-moving boat.

- **striking**   Here, the reference is to fish taking the bait.

- **shot**   buckshot.

- **the ventral fin**   A fin situated on or close to the abdomen of a fish.

"THE THREE-DAY BLOW"

Summary

One rainy autumn afternoon, Nick hikes up in the north Michigan woods to a cabin to meet his friend Bill. Talking and drinking, they finally discuss Nick's breaking off his romantic relationship with Marjorie. Bill dogmatically insists that Nick did the right thing. A woman, he insists, will ruin a man; a married man is "done for." Nick listens but realizes that he is still free to flirt with the idea of finding the right woman to marry eventually. He is far from being converted to Bill's almost misogynistic view of women.

Commentary

This story is the sequel, or follow up, to "The End of Something." Bill, who emerged only briefly in the earlier story, plays a major role here. The setting is a cabin in the north Michigan woods that belongs to Bill's father and sits high above the lake with a good view of the woods. The time is fall, just before the first big autumn storm blows in.

As Nick hikes upward, approaching the cabin, Hemingway precisely places him in the narrative, and his sharp attention to details is characteristic of Hemingway's early prose as well as his later, long narratives. Nick picks up a "Wagner apple." He puts it in the pocket of his "Mackinaw coat."

Almost immediately, Bill offers Nick a drink—and from this point onward, we watch and listen as the two young men get increasingly drunk. Bill is clearly in charge. Because of the cold, rainy autumn weather, he chides Nick for not wearing any socks and goes upstairs to get him some. He also cautions Nick about denting the fireplace screen with his feet (biographers have often noted Hemingway's big feet. Knowing his fondness for inserting autobiographical material, this small, telling detail very likely happened).

Besides the reference to big feet, Bill calls Nick "Wemedge," a nickname Hemingway chose for himself. The two guys settle into a not-quite-comfortable camaraderie, joshing about baseball. Bill is careful to keep their talk light, for the moment.

The tension between the two young men, however, is unrelieved by liquor or by the talk of baseball; the two begin discussing books. Biographers have noted that when Hemingway wrote this short story, he and his friend Bill Smith were reading the same books that Hemingway mentions here in the story. Again, Bill must take charge, controlling the flow of conversation. Frustrated by the small talk, Bill suggests getting drunk.

When Nick insists that he's already a little drunk, Bill is direct: "You aren't drunk." Clearly, he wants to get them both drunk enough to talk about what's really on both of their minds.

Finally, Bill shifts to the real subject: Nick's breaking off with Marjorie. We see now that it was Bill who talked Nick into breaking up with her. Bill begins railing against the whole notion of marriage. Women, he contends, ruin a man; a married man is "done for." Sitting quietly, Nick realizes how much he lost when he broke off with Marjorie. His guilt is keen. Bill feels no guilt for his part in the breaking-up. "So long as it's over that's all that matters," he pronounces. Further, Bill cautions Nick to watch himself and not succumb to temptation again.

Nick, however, realizes that all is not over. The notion of there being danger in falling for Marjorie, or any other woman, is still possible. He hasn't cut himself off from the possibility of romance. The danger intrigues him; he's thrilled with the concept that danger isn't a bad thing.

Marjorie threatened Bill's friendship with Nick, which Bill admits: Had Nick not broken off with Marjorie, he'd already be living in Charlevoix to be near her. Hunting, fishing, and drinking, according to Bill, are more important than getting married. Nick, however, felt anchored somehow with Marjorie, as if life had a purpose and a pattern. At the end of the story, he's doubly exhilarated: He's happy to be hunting with Bill, and he's excited that a relationship with a woman, even if it might seem to trap him, is always waiting for him. The emotional high he feels because of this new insight is bracing.

- **Mackinaw coat**　a short, double-breasted coat of heavy, plaid woolen material.

- **peat**　decayed, partly decomposed grass and weeds matter found in bogs; it is used for fertilizer.

- **the Giants**　the New York Giants, a Major League baseball team from 1902-32.

- **McGraw**　John J. McCraw, manager of the New York Giants.

- **Heinie Zim**　Heinie Zimmerman, a Chicago Cubs baseball player; he was traded to the New York Giants.

- *Richard Feverel*　an 1859 novel by the British author George Meredith.

- *Forest Lovers*　a novel written by Maurice Hewlitt and published in 1898. In the story, Bill has recommended that Nick read this novel, whose plot includes a young man breaking off his relationship with a girl of lesser social status.

- *The Dark Forest*　a novel by the British author Horace Walpole.

- **Chesterton**　G. K. Chesterton, a British novelist and poet.

- **Voix**　The reference is to the town of Charlevoix, located in northern Michigan.

- **louts**　awkward and stupid people.

"THE KILLERS"

Summary

One winter evening, around dusk, while he is sitting at the end of a counter and talking to George, the manager of a diner in Summit, Illinois, a small town south of Chicago, Nick Adams watches two over-dressed strangers in black (Al and Max) enter the diner. After complaining about the serving schedule, the two men order dinner, joking sarcastically about George and Nick being a couple of dumb country boys.

Finishing his meal, Al orders Nick and Sam, the Black cook, to the kitchen, where he ties them up. Meanwhile, Max boasts to George that he and Al have been hired to kill Ole Andreson, an aging boxer, who, they've heard, eats dinner there every night.

When the boxer fails to show up in the diner, Al and Max leave, and George hurries to untie Nick and Sam. He then suggests that Nick warn Andreson, who lives in a nearby boarding house.

When the boxer hears about Al and Max's plan to kill him, he's unconcerned; he's tired, he says, of running. Nick leaves and returns to the diner, where he tells George and Sam that he's leaving Summit because he can't bear to think about a man waiting, passively, to be killed by a couple of hired killers.

Commentary

In the 1940s, when Hemingway's stories were beginning to be anthologized, "Indian Camp" and "The Killers" were the two stories most often published in textbooks and literary anthologies.

Pervading this short story is an overwhelming mood of bleakness. The setting is a lunch counter diner, located in a small town, ironically called Summit, some miles from Chicago, Illinois. After Andreson's usual eating time has passed, the killers leave, and George tells Nick that he should warn Andreson. In Ole's rented room, Ole seems undisturbed by the news; in fact, he seems as though he almost expected to hear about the plan to kill him. He tells Nick that he can't run any longer and that nothing can be done about his situation. He sends Nick away.

Interestingly, Ole is lying in his bed turned toward the wall in his room as he waits for his death; in "Indian Camp," the young American Indian husband slits his throat while he is turned toward the wall lying in his bunk.

Map Explanation

Summit, Illinois, is the setting for Hemingway's "The Killers."
Nick Adams is living in Summit, leading what seems to be an un-
eventful life, when he is suddenly confronted by two hired killers,
probably from Chicago, who intend to murder a professional boxer,
Ole Andreson. Nick rushes to Andreson's boarding house and tells
him that he is marked as a target by the killers and Andreson says
that he's tired of running, that he'll wait for the killers; Nick leaves
Summit, sickened in disbelief that a man can passively await his
own, certain death.

Returning back to the diner, Nick begins telling George and the cook (who goes into the kitchen so he won't have to hear anything more about the murder that's being planned) what happened in Ole's apartment. Nick says that he's going to leave town because being in a town where a man passively awaits being gunned down is too terrible. Nick "can't stand . . . it." In "Indian Camp," Nick's father made a grave distinction between men who succumbed to fear and couldn't face dire adversity. They became suicidal weaklings: the ones who "couldn't stand things." As a small boy, Nick vowed never to be one of these men.

Ironically, Hemingway's story is not about "the killers," nor is it about Ole Andreson, the prizefighter who it is assumed is killed. Rather, the story is about Nick Adams' confrontation with unmitigated evil, represented by the two gangsters, Al and Max.

Note that we don't even know why the killers are murdering Andreson; George thinks that the prizefighter must have betrayed or double-crossed some gamblers. Ole simply says to Nick that he "got in wrong." The main concern, however, has little to do with Andreson or the killers. Readers are far more concerned with Nick Adams' initiation, or exposure, to evil and how he reacts to it.

Hemingway uses no subtlety in characterizing Al and Max. They clearly represent the epitome of evil, almost as though they stepped out of a medieval morality play. Their faces are not alike, yet they are dressed in identical black overcoats, and black gloves—black, of course, being the most common and perhaps oldest symbol of evil.

Seemingly, this episode in the diner is Nick Adams' first encounter with evil—killing done simply for the sake of killing by men hired to kill, who have no family, business, or emotional ties to their victim. Neither Al nor Max has even met Andreson, yet they plan to kill him coldly and impersonally. Nick's deep sense of responsibility is evident in his need to warn Andreson of the impending danger, and he is confused by Andreson's passive attitude.

Considering the different kinds of reactions to evil, first there is the cook's reaction, who wants to close his eyes to the existence of evil, to close his ears to it, and to pretend that it isn't there, hearing no more about it. Then there is George, who recognizes that evil exists but yet sends someone else (Nick, in this case) to deal with it. Also, there is Andreson; he succumbs to the inevitable that is his fate. Finally, Nick Adams recognizes the horror of evil and attempts to do something about it, but when he cannot, he yearns to run away. Although he responds to evil and wants to do something about it, upon witnessing Ole doing absolutely nothing about it himself, Nick decides to leave town and ultimately surrenders to the threat of evil himself.

Like the American Indian husband in "Indian Camp, a man who "couldn't stand" his wife's suffering, so Nick "can't stand" Ole Andreson's waiting in his room and "knowing that he is going to get it."

Additionally, Nick also learns that the world is not always what it seems. For instance, the diner was built as a bar (and still has some of the acoutrements); the clock and the menu don't reflect what time it is and what is being served; the killers look a little like Laurel and Hardy, although they are dressed in black; the boarding house owner is absent.

Nick is also exposed to the heavyweight fighter who once fought for money but now refuses to fight—even for his life. Andreson clearly knows that the hired killers are going to murder him, but he has lost the will to fight. Ole, a prizefighter, isn't a fighter; and Nick isn't able to confront the evil as he thought he could. This attitude is, of course, antithetical to the values of what would develop as Hemingway's standard code hero; a man who must recognize death as the end of everything and must therefore struggle against this final nothingness.

Fleeing evil is not an option for the typical code hero of Hemingway's later fiction. A man must confront evil—or, in this case, Andreson's inevitable death—and he must try to understand it. Running from evil is as much a violation of the code hero's persona as suicide is. How one reacts to evil is ultimately more important than the evil itself.

- **wicket**   here, a small gate separating the kitchen from the dining room of the diner.

- **kosher convent**   To most people, a convent is associated with Catholicism; here, Max jokes that Al, probably Jewish, would have to be in a "kosher" convent; kosher is Yiddish for food that is ritually clean, according to dietary laws.

- **muzzle of a sawed-off shotgun**   the firing end of the gun.

- **the car-tracks**   The reference is to electric streetcar tracks.

"A WAY YOU'LL NEVER BE"

Summary

Nick Adams has been wounded in Italy during World War I and is suffering from shell-shock, or post-traumatic stress syndrome. He is plagued by nightmares, in which he sees the eyes of the Austrian soldier who shot him. Nick's friend, the Italian Captain Paravicini, believes that Nick's head wound should have been treated differently; he worries about Nick's bouts of "craziness."

One hot summer day, Nick bicycles from the village of Fornaci to Captain Paravicini's encampment. On the way, he witnesses the miles of bloated corpses and the hundreds of blowing pieces of military papers.

When Nick reaches camp, an Italian second lieutenant questions Nick's identification papers before Paravicini intervenes and coaxes Nick to lie down and rest before he returns to Fornaci; he fears for Nick's sanity and safety despite the young American's valiant attempt to deal with his war-torn memories.

Commentary

Here, Hemingway has written what is essentially an account—sometimes realistic, sometimes impressionistic, and sometimes plainly confusing—of Nick Adams' coping with post-traumatic trauma and possibly a concussion suffered in battle during World War I.

As he is riding his bicycle along the Austro-Italian front in northern Italy, Nick sees scattered evidence of the ravages of war, described in a surrealistic manner: Pornographic cards are scattered among the dead bodies of Italian soldiers that have never been buried. The heat-swollen, rotting bodies have been stripped of anything of value, as have the corpses of the Austrian soldiers.

This setting—the Austro-Italian border—is an area that Hemingway knew well. As a volunteer Red Cross ambulance driver, he was often bored because there were no battles in which he could prove his heroism. As a result, he volunteered to help staff one of several supply centers, from which he'd take chocolate, cigarettes, and postcards to men on the front lines.

When Nick arrives at the encampment, he tells the battalion commander that he "should have a musette of chocolate . . . [but] there weren't any cigarettes and postcards and no chocolate." Nick's role here is clearly autobiographical. What is not autobiographical, however, is Nick's head injury and his mental anguish. Hemingway suffered severe leg and thigh wounds on just such an errand as Nick is doing.

Nick also suffers from the severe heat. Early in the story, he notes how the heat has humped and swollen the bodies of the dead soldiers. The sun causes "heat-waves in the air above the leaves where [it] hit . . . guns hidden in mulberry hedges." When Nick readies himself to return to the supply center camp, Captain Paravicini cautions him that "it is still hot to ride."

One of the keys to understanding this confusing, short sketch is Hemingway's focus on Nick's identity. Nick is officially questioned when he reaches the battalion of Italian soldiers camped along the Piave River. The soldier who reads Nick's identification card is clearly not convinced that Nick is a bona fide soldier despite the fact that Nick says that he knows the Italian soldier's captain. Nick does indeed know Captain Paravicini—for the same reason that Hemingway took pleasure in making friends with high-ranking Italian officers: American Red Cross volunteers were free to fraternize with Italian officers.

Although glad to talk to the captain about the success of the last attack, Nick is self-conscious and restless. He's aware that the captain knows that Nick's head wound and battle trauma have changed him, and thus he uses humor to keep their talk from centering too keenly on himself.

The captain, however, sees through the ruse and joshes Nick about his preposterous tale that he is a decoy, dressed—albeit a bit flawed—like an American so that the Austrians will conclude that at any moment, millions of American soldiers—brave and clean—will suddenly burst onto the battlefield and decimate the Austrians.

The muddled stream-of-consciousness technique that Hemingway uses to describe Nick's dream is a rare instance of his using this particular narrative technique. His writing style is usually characterized by short, crisp declarative sentences. The technique here is remarkably different.

According to Carlos Baker's biography of Hemingway, the title of this short story comes from a situation in Cuba; the heat was intense, and Hemingway remarked that it reminded him of the way it was on the lower Piave in the summer of 1918, while he was watching "a hell of a nice girl going crazy from day to day." Hemingway borrowed pieces of this girl's madness for Nick's confused behavior; for example, as Nick is leaving the captain, he feels another attack of confusion coming on: "He felt it coming on again. . . . He was trying to hold it in. . . . He knew he could not stop it now."

Many of Hemingway's novels and writings would focus on physical wounds and on the death and blood in this story. However, Hemingway also focuses on wounds unseen—the psychological results of war and the effect of a head wound on Nick Adams, a subject that he would return to in "Big Two-Hearted River."

- **the attack** The setting of this story is northern Italy during World War I; an Italian town has been attacked by an Austrian military offensive.

- **haversacks** bags carried over only one shoulder to transport supplies.

- **stick bombs** hand grenades with handles.

- **mustard gas** an oily, highly flammable liquid; it was used during World War I as a chemical weapon.

- **shrapnel** an artillery shell filled with metal balls that explode in the air and rip into flesh.

"IN ANOTHER COUNTRY"

Summary

Trying to regain use of a knee that was wounded during World War I, Nick is in an Italian hospital for therapy, riding a kind of tricycle that his doctor promises will keep the muscles elastic. Nick is dubious of the machine and the therapy, as is a friend of his, an Italian major who is also undergoing therapy with a machine that exercises his hand that was injured in an industrial accident.

Four other young men, Italian soldiers, are also using therapy machines, and they brag about the medals that they've received for their valor in battle. In contrast, the major never brags about his own bravery. He is deeply depressed and finally reveals to Nick that his young wife has just died.

Commentary

As noted elsewhere, the Nick Adams stories were not published in chronological order, paralleling Nick Adams' maturing from a small boy to a mature adult. This story, for instance, appeared in the 1927 issue of *Scribner's* magazine, some two to four years *after* "Indian Camp," the first of the Nick Adams stories to appear. Here, the narrator is unnamed, and early critics didn't associate this narrator with Nick Adams, but subsequent critics agree that the main character is indeed the Nick Adams of the other stories, the Nick Adams who will go to the Big Two-Hearted River to fish and forget his war experiences and try to heal his physical and psychological wounds.

When the story was first published, many readers were puzzled about what this story was about. Later critics have even wondered if this is the major's story or the narrator's story. Read within the context of the other Nick Adams stories, this question is easily solved. "In Another Country" is, of course, a Nick Adams story. From the other stories, we realize that Nick Adams is honest, virile, and, more important, a person of extreme sensitivity. By observing the particular state of mind of the young narrator at the beginning of the story, we see that what happens to the major makes a tremendous impact on the young, wounded soldier.

The narrator's sensitivity is keenly presented by the way in which he observes his surroundings. It begins with one of Hemingway's simple, perfect sentences—a sentence that could not have been written by anyone else: "In the fall the war was always there, but we did not go to it any more."

Other observations in the first paragraph reveal the narrator's extremely sensitive mind making sharp observations: "There was much game hanging outside the shops, and the snow powdered in the fur of the foxes and the wind blew their tails. The deer hung stiff and heavy and empty . . ." or "On one of [the bridges], a woman sold roasted chestnuts. It was warm, standing in front of her charcoal fire, and the chestnuts were warm afterwards in your pockets." The descriptions are so vivid that we are often lulled into a complacency and do not realize that the story is really about bravery, courage, and death.

Map Explanation

Using Italy as the setting for "A Way You'll Never Be" and "In Another Country," Hemingway explores the experience and the effect of war as seen through the eyes of the central character, Nick Adams.

"A Way You'll Never Be" concentrates on Nick's head wound and the effects of heat, concussion, and psychological trauma while near the Austro-Italian border shortly after the war. It is an account of how Nick copes with shell shock, or what is known today as post-traumatic stress syndrome, and the visual reminders and residue of death, destruction, and loss. Seeing the bodies of the Italians and Austrians piled up and rotting in the heat in Italy becomes an inescapable image for Nick.

One notable characteristic about this short literary sketch is how Hemingway uses a different writing technique from his own to create Nick's dream. Hemingway's style is lean and declarative; in Nick's dream, the style is different, creating a surreal dreamscape that separates the "Hemingway reality" seen in his usual sparkling, clear style.

"In Another Country" revisits the Hemingway code hero concept, with Nick Adams recuperating in an Italian hospital alongside some high-ranking Italian officers and a friend who is a major. They are all resting and undergoing physical therapy. While there, Nick observes the behavior of his older and higher-ranking friend, the major. It is this particular man that Nick identifies with and learns from by observing how he reacts to other mens' bragging, personal loss, and physical therapy itself. Additionally, Nick learns what it is to be disciplined, even if he does not entirely believe in what he is doing.

Structurally, Hemingway creates three recurrent ideas: Nick's break with society; the subsequent establishment of his "code"; and the wound, which influences the first two factors. Nick's wound, while not always displayed or talked about, nevertheless plays a central role in this story. Nick will be the prototype for many of Hemingway's later characters. Wounded, Nick feels that the three Italians with medals are "hunting hawks," men who lived by the importance attached to their medals. In contrast, the major who has many medals never talks about them. Additionally, Nick feels that he has not served as a participant in the war. He feels alienated from the three "hawks" and aligns himself with the young soldier who was wounded in the face, who was not at the front "long enough to be tested."

The first half of this very short story deals mostly with the setting and other observations and creates an atmosphere of alienation, one directly related to Nick's own sense of insecurity. Then the story shifts, and we meet the major, undergoing physical therapy and using a machine nearby the machine that Nick is using. The major represents the older, established "code hero"; Nick is the initiate who will learn from the major's reactions to war, to the machines, and to death. Like many future Hemingway heroes, the major has been at the top of his craft; he was once the finest fencer in Italy, but now his fencing hand is wounded, stunted, and withered. Furthermore, the major has been awarded three medals and yet never mentions them because he does not believe in touting bravery.

In contrast to the three young "hawks" who brag about their medals, Nick doesn't feel comfortable bragging about his medals. He is drawn to the major, who is obviously a brave man but doesn't talk about it. Furthermore, the major does not believe in the so-called therapeutic success of the machines, yet he continues to come to the hospital and use them. Nick does not understand this contradiction at first because, for the major, the machines represent a discipline that is necessary for the Hemingway code hero. In a similar way, the major insists that Nick speak Italian that is grammatically correct. This is another type of discipline, and the major spends a good deal of time correcting Nick's grammar.

The major is sardonic about doctors; his comments are filled with veiled contempt. When a doctor tells Nick that he will play football again, the major wants to know if he too will ever play football again. The major, once Italy's greatest fencer, is honest and realistic about the therapeutic value of the machines and points out that if he and Nick are the first to use them, where did the doctor get the "before and after" pictures?

When the major bursts out into a vindictive attack against marriage, Nick is caught off balance by the major's intense, emotional explosion because the major has usually exhibited superbly disciplined control of himself. Readers later learn that the major's wife, much younger than he, has just died from pneumonia after three days of suffering. The major cannot resign himself to the loss of his wife. He is crushed, shattered by the news.

This story combines two of Hemingway's favorite narrative devices: First, he creates an older, seasoned code hero, a man who has confronted life and has experienced the hard, cruel world but has not given in to any display of emotion; he has carefully refrained from baring his emotions except in this very rare case of the death of his young wife. He never talks of his own bravery or his courage or his exploits on the battlefield; he lives a highly disciplined life until he has to confront the death of his wife.

Second, in contrast to the older code character, we have the initiate—here, young Nick Adams, the innocent soldier who is just entering into a world of war and violence.

- **in the fall**   possibly an autumn during 1918, the last year of World War I. Hemingway was injured in July 1918 while delivering chocolates and cigarettes to Italian soldiers stationed on the Piave River.

- **a black band**   the black cloth band that the major wears around the upper part of his arm of his uniform, signifying that he is in mourning.

"BIG TWO-HEARTED RIVER: PART I"

Summary

Emotionally wounded and disillusioned by World War I, Nick Adams returns to his home and leaves for the north Michigan woods on a camping trip. He leaves by himself, hoping that the routine of selecting a good place to camp, setting up a tent, fixing meals, and preparing for fishing will restore peace and a sense of balance to his traumatized soul.

On the way to the woods, Nick passes the ruined, gutted, burned-to-the-ground town of Seney. The first half of this solitary sojourn focuses on passing through Seney and setting up camp, which comprises Part I.

Commentary

According to Hemingway biographer James R. Mellon, Hemingway regarded "Big Two-Hearted River" as the "climactic story in [his short story collection] *In Our Time* and the culminating episode in the Nick Adams adventures that he included in the book."

That comment ought to spark the curiosity of readers of this story, for, on the surface, very little happens in the story. Seemingly, it goes nowhere. If, however, one has read Thoreau's *Walden*, it is relatively easy to see that Hemingway is portraying Nick Adams' attempt to achieve a bonding with nature that Thoreau, in 1845, was seeking when he decided to live a simple, semi-solitary life at Walden Pond. In *Walden*, Thoreau says: "I went to the woods because I wished to live deliberately . . . and see if I could learn what it had to teach. . . . I wanted to live deep and suck out all the marrow of life."

This "living deliberately" is the key to what Nick is seeking through the restorative and recuperative powers of nature. He has seen first-hand the horrors of war (World War I), was seriously injured himself and suffered a mental breakdown. He is searching for some way to put the horrors of these experiences behind him and restore himself to a healthy emotional life. To do so, he feels that he must isolate himself from the rest of humanity until he regains his own sense of sanity and humanity.

Interestingly, trout fishing plays an important role for many of Hemingway's male characters. For example, in *The Sun Also Rises*, the main character, Jake Barnes, who, like Nick, was seriously wounded in the war, goes with his best friend to the Spanish Mountains for some trout fishing, especially when he is about to lose control of his life. Ultimately, the traditional Christian symbols of fishing and water become symbolic of Nick's being rebaptized into life. However, even though two prominent Western world symbols have been mentioned thus far, this is not a story whose meaning relies on symbols. Instead, it is a realistic account of a fishing trip during which Nick regains control of his life.

Two major, over-arching themes can be seen in each part: recovery in Part I and recollection in Part II.

Part I Commentary

Nick's recovery begins here as Nick goes alone to a deserted area along the fictional Two-Hearted River (Michigan's Fox River) in the upper peninsula of northern Michigan, where he can see Lake Superior from a hilltop, where "there was no town, nothing but the rails and the burned-over country. . . . It was all that was left of the town of Seney." The symbolism here is fairly obvious: Nick is leaving the burned, destroyed portions of his life behind, hoping and searching for renewal on the rich, green, and fertile river bank of the big Two-Hearted River. Nick, however, does not go immediately to the river; instead, he gets off the train and pauses on a bridge, watching trout that are far below him in the stream. It is important to note here that Nick is looking down onto the river and the trout, which will both be living, breathing symbols that are essential to Nick's healing later. The trout are all steadily floating in deep, fast-moving water. Hemingway uses another important symbol here: the kingfisher, a brightly-colored bird that dives just under the water's surface for fish. This is most definitely a metaphor for the facile, healthy spiritual state that Nick is seeking on this solitary camping trip. The bird's ability to fly is a traditional symbol for spiritual ascension and the ability to transgress beyond worldly cares, and the bird's ability to go underneath the surface and pluck things out of the river and digest them is a metaphor for what Nick needs to do to transmutate his unpleasant memories. He follows the river from a distance, for some time, delaying gratification before deciding on a place for his camp. He wants to begin his healing in the woods deliberately and with discipline. Throughout the story, he will be isolated from other people. He will not see or communicate with anyone.

Map Explanation

The northern peninsula of Michigan is the setting for many of Hemingway's Nick Adams stories: "Indian Camp," "The Doctor and the Doctor's Wife," "The End of Something," "The Three-Day Blow," and Parts I and II of "Big Two-Hearted River." This country was intensely familiar to Hemingway; he grew up fishing, hunting, hiking, and camping along the rivers and in the woods and hills of this region.

Horton Bay, in "The End of Something," is referred to as Hortons Bay; today, the once-burned-out town of Seney has been rebuilt. In "The Three-Day Blow," Bill tells Nick Adams that had Nick continued dating Marjorie, he would not be drinking scotch with Bill in the cabin; he'd be living a boring, middle-class life with Marjorie in Charlevoix; Nick reluctantly agrees.

After Nick is wounded, physically and psychologically, during his stint as a soldier in Italy during World War I, he returns to the woods of northern Michigan and camps along the Two-Hearted River, fishing for trout and slowly restoring serenity and peace to his broken mind and emotions.

Hemingway's father had a summer cabin, Windemere, here in the northern peninsula; it was along the streams and rivers, where they fished and camped, that Dr. Hemingway taught his son the skills and codes of life—especially living outdoors, independently, on one's own.

When he sees the trout moving about in the pools of the river, he feels an elation that he has not felt for a long time. Nick saw trout in the stream below the bridge; his "heart tightened as the trout moved." Then, leaving the burned town behind him, Nick "felt happy. He felt he had left everything behind, the need for thinking, the need to write, other needs. It was all back of him." These key ideas, then, are the essence of this story: Nick has escaped into his own world where the mere sight of trout influences his responses. He is at one with this world: "He did not need to get his map out. He knew where he was from the position of the river."

As Nick walks through Seney, he notices that even the surface of the ground has been burned. The black, sooty ruin of Seney represents the atrocities of war and its devastating effect on Nick's psycho-emotional well being. Here, he walks through it and notices that even the grasshoppers are covered with soot, much the same way that Nick himself is still covered with "soot" from the war.

However, note that Nick does not go to the river immediately. He wants to get as far upstream as he can in one day's walking. Even though he stops and instinctively knows that the river cannot be more than a mile north of where he is, being tired, he takes off his backpack and sleeps on the ground until the sun is almost down.

The description of Nick's putting up the tent, smoothing the ground, chopping stakes, pulling the tent taut, hanging cheesecloth over the front—all of these components coalesce and make Nick feel happy: "He had made his camp. He was settled. Nothing could touch him. It was a good place to camp."

Hemingway is famous for avoiding three-syllable, high-flown adjectives; instead, he uses simple adjectives such as "good." Here, this was a "good place" to camp.

Afterward, Nick makes his supper—a can of pork and beans mixed with a can of spaghetti. As the two ingredients cook together, Nick inhales a "good" smell—not a "superb aroma"—just simply a "good" smell.

Nick is trying to return to basics, to regain a sense of the simplicity of life; thus Hemingway presents his camping trip in its simplest terms. Even though Nick eats plain, canned food, he describes it lovingly: " . . . he had been that hungry before, but had not been able to satisfy it." His hunger is satisfied both literally and metaphorically. And again, he pronounces his camp "good." Later, Nick again asserts that there "were plenty of good places to camp on the river. But this was good."

Hemingway presents a moving picture of Nick making camp with meticulous, detailed descriptions that add a methodical, ritualized dimension. It is this solitary, repetitive, methodical action of making camp that frees Nick's mind from stress, bad memories, and the cares of the world. It is a moving meditation unto itself, providing Nick with a mind-numbing and pain-relieving sense of calm and relaxation. Nick's own moving meditation here in the woods is no different from the traditional Eastern image of the spiritual seeker who sits on a mountaintop, chanting "om" and other mantras while in deep meditation.

Thought and grief are inexorably linked in Nick's mind now, and this moving meditation heals him.

Nick then turns his focus on making camp coffee; he remembers a guy named Hopkins, who considered himself an expert on making camp coffee. We know no more about this person than is presented in this single paragraph, but the mood of the paragraph invokes a sense of "long ago," in stark contrast to the very vivid "now" that Nick is creating for himself. Then, long ago, Nick and Bill and Hopkins were young and joyous, carefree, and dreamily optimistic. Their youthful days of irresponsibility were broken, however, when Hopkins received a telegram informing him that he was suddenly very rich; back in Texas, his first big oil well had hit pay dirt. Hopkins immediately promised his two buddies that he'd take them sailing on the yacht that he was going to buy. Nick never heard from Hopkins again.

The implication is that Hopkins was swallowed by the world of money and materialism and forgot about such basic values as friendship. Similarly, Nick once believed in the glory of war and was almost killed by the machines of war, yet he survived and has come "home" to nature to restore his physical and mental health.

The dinner and the ritualistic way Nick drinks his coffee in the "Hopkins" manner put Nick back in touch with past friends and associations that bring back some good memories.

The last two paragraphs of Part I conclude with Nick's preparation for sleep, as he crawls into his tent and feels sleep coming. This concludes the first of two major, over-arching themes in the story: the period of recollection for Nick, as it encompasses the war, good memories prior to the war, and connects Nick to Nature itself. Nature is a living, breathing, presence that Nick merges with to move beyond stress and ill health back to good health and creativity. It is a quiet and peaceful break that firmly cements the first theme before Nick enters into the world of the river and fishing in Part II.

- **burnt timber**   The reference is to the forest fire that destroyed vast acres of woodland, as well as the town of Seney, Michigan.

- **convex**   having a surface that bulges outward.

- **cinders**   burned remains.

- **jack pines**   North American evergreens with soft wood and short, twisted needles.

- **swale**   a slightly lower tract of land either created or caused by running water.

- **cheesecloth**   coarsely, loosely woven gauze.

"BIG TWO-HEARTED RIVER: PART II"

Summary

Hemingway recounts in precise detail Nick's rituals of preparation for fishing before he wades into the river. He successfully catches two trout and begins to gather sufficient courage so that in the days ahead, he can easily fish across the river, in the dark swamp, a symbol of Nick's fears and uncertainties. Clearly, Nick's recovery from the trauma of war has already begun, and readers finish this story with a sense of hope.

Commentary

This section presents Nick's preparations for fishing and his actual wading into the river to fish for trout and examines his accompanying emotions and reactions. Every detail, every action, is understated. Hemingway describes no grandiose epiphanies. The river is the central element in this section, as Nick is constantly in the river, following the river, and looking to the swamp at the end of the river. The river is a consistent thread here that parallels Nick's subconscious and the memories contained therein.

First, Nick must have some bait. He is surrounded by grasshoppers, and luckily, they are sluggish this early in the morning because of the heavy dew. Nick gets an empty bottle and collects enough bait for the entire day; he knows that he can get all the "hoppers" he needs each morning of each day for the rest of his stay in the woods. It is important here to note the contrast between the grasshoppers in Part I, which were black and covered with soot, and these grasshoppers, which are nestled in the grass amongst the drops of dew, waiting for the sun. If the river is Nick's subconscious, then the grasshoppers represent the mundane, methodical camping tasks that are calming to Nick and enable him to dip into his subconscious without fear, much like the kingfisher in Part I.

Nick retrieves his fishing rod from the leather rod case and prepares the leader line, the gut line, and the hook, and tests them: "It was a good feeling."

All preparations completed, Nick is ready to enter the water. As he leaves camp, he feels "awkward" but "professionally happy" with all of his paraphernalia hanging from him: His sandwiches are in his two front pockets; his bottle of grasshoppers is hanging around his neck; his landing net is hanging from a hook in his belt; a long flour sack is tied round his shoulder (this will hold the trout that he catches); his "fly book" is in one of his pockets; and he is carrying his fly rod.

Nick's first catch is too small, so he removes the hook and throws it back. Note that before he touches the trout, he wets his hand because he knows that "if a trout was touched with a dry hand, a white fungus attacked the unprotected spot." This kind of knowledge emphasizes again that Nick is an expert in this type of fishing; readers respect him. However, it also indicates something deeper: Nick has a specific code of fishing that separates him from other fishermen. It places Nick into a select, morally "higher" group that respects the fish and Nature. This totally integrates Nick with the fish and Nature itself.

Nick then rebaits his hook and, this time, spits on it for good luck, a typical thing for an experienced fisherman to do. This time, and it does not take long, he hooks an enormous trout: When it leaps high out of the water, Nick is overcome because he has never seen such a large trout, but then "tragedy" strikes: The leader line breaks, and the trout escapes.

Nick's hand is shaking. He slowly reels in his empty hook. He vaguely feels a little sick, as though it would be better to sit down.

These details illustrate Hemingway's belief that if people—men, in particular—give in to their emotions, they are in danger of losing everything. For Nick, the thrill of hooking this large trout is overwhelming. Some may also surmise that the trout represent happy memories, and that this big trophy trout that gets away is a symbol for a memory that made Nick very happy but didn't come to fruition for whatever reason. The emotional investment in something that makes him happy that he ultimately can't connect with again at this point in his recovery is a sickening disappointment to him, especially because it's his fault. However, after the jarring experience of war, Nick must expect to "lose a few" at first during his journey into his own river of recovery.

After he rests and smokes, Nick rebaits, and this time, upon reentering the river, he works his rod carefully. He catches a good-sized trout, and note that he says that it was "good" to hold—he had "one good trout." Nick catches another, but for the second time, the trout gets away, although this time, it isn't Nick's fault. The fish dives into heavy underbrush.

Almost immediately, Nick has another strike, and after some struggling, he brings this trout into his net. Nick then spreads the "mouth of the sack and [looks] down at the two big trout alive in the water." He concludes that they are good trout.

After Nick eats his sandwiches, he sits and watches the river; then he kills and dresses the two trout. Both are males because each is exuding "milt," a substance found only in male fish. Nick returns to camp completely satisfied and looks forward to the days to come when he will fish the swampy areas, as he steadily moved downstream into deeper water today.

Nick's steady progress downstream into deeper water leads him to reach a point in the river that intersects the present moment: His wish for something to read. This return to thinking and cerebral pursuits indicates a mental rejuvenation. It isn't a total rejuvenation, because Nick has yet to fish in the swamp, but it is a rejuvenation that indicates to the reader that Nick's recovery is well underway.

Another signpost of Nick's progress in recovery is his emotional reaction to swamp fishing. The swamp is a deep, dark place at the end of the river covered by cedar branches. It is a dangerous place to fish because of the muck on the bottom and the fast, deep water that sometimes has whirlpools that take anything in the water down with it. It is here that the really big trout seek the shade and cool water, and it is here that Nick reacts to it: first, by concluding that he won't do it just yet, and second, that it is "tragic," which is an emotionally charged description. The swamp can be seen as the dark, sooty place in Nick's subconscious where the war and all of the bad memories from it reside. For Nick, this swamp (and swamp fishing) is the final frontier of healing and transmutating the war experience. It is no surprise that he concludes that he will try it another time, without any reference to a timetable or a goal for doing it. He is satisfied with his present progress, and he'll simply do it when it occurs to him that he is ready.

After having followed Nick through his two days in the woods by the river, readers are filled with confidence that Nick is a survivor and that he will be able to put all of the horrors of the war behind and find a suitable niche in life.

- **condensed milk**   canned milk.
- **a fly**   an artificial fishing lure, often resembling an insect.
- **leaders**   lengths of wire or gut or nylon connecting hooks to fishing lines.
- **milt**   fish sperm, along with seminal fluid.
- **offal**   intestines or waste parts of butchered fish.

OTHER WELL-KNOWN HEMINGWAY SHORT STORIES

"THE SHORT HAPPY LIFE OF FRANCIS MACOMBER"

Summary

It is noon. Francis Macomber is on an African safari; Macomber is thirty-five years old, a trim, fit man who holds a number of big-game fishing records. However, at the moment, he has just demonstrated that he is a coward. However, members of the safari are acting as though "nothing had happened." The natives at camp carried Macomber into camp triumphantly, but the gun-bearers who witnessed Macomber's cowardice do not participate in the celebration.

In a flashback, the reader realizes that Macomber and his beautiful wife, Margot, are wealthy Americans, and that this jaunt is their first safari—and that Macomber, when faced with his first lion, bolted and fled, earning the contempt of his wife. Of course, though, she has been contemptuous of him for some time; Francis' running from the lion like a scared rabbit has only increased her dislike for her unmanly husband. She makes no secret of this as she slips off in the middle of the night for a rendezvous with the safari guide, Robert Wilson.

Next day, as she observes Francis gaining a measure of courage as he engages in a standoff with a charging water buffalo, she realizes that if Francis continues to prove himself strong and willful and courageous, he might leave her and rid himself forever of her sharp-tongued ridicule.

As the standoff with the second water buffalo becomes more intense as the water buffalo's horns inch closer and closer to goring Francis, Margot takes aim at the water buffalo, shooting Francis in the back of the head, and he dies at the most courageous moment of his "short happy life."

Commentary

In the first part of this story, readers hear all sorts of things that have meaning only later in the story. For example, Margot points out that the face of Robert Wilson, the safari guide, is red (from too much sun); Francis Macomber replies that his face is also red; however, his is red from embarrassment. In contrast to the two men, Margo comments that her face is the one that is red today because of all the shame she feels for her husband.

Behind all of this talk about red faces, however, is the fact that after Francis' act of cowardice, Margot leans forward in their motor car and kisses Wilson while Macomber looks on. That night, Margot visits Wilson's tent and has sex with him. Interestingly, Hemingway points out that Wilson always carries a double-size cot for just such occasions as this one; obviously, Wilson is a womanizer and in a sense a prostitute.

In this story, the situation of the hunter and the hunted takes on far more significance than merely humans hunting for African lions and water buffaloes. Consider who is stalking whom in this story. Francis knows that Margot is stalking Wilson, and Wilson realizes that Francis knows who Margot's prey is. Francis Macomber even admits that he feels "beaten," defeated by this sexual safari, because when Wilson explains that he always gives the natives lashes rather than fine them, Macomber adds that "We all take a beating every day . . . one way or another."

Hemingway's sympathy in this story is not with the victim Macomber or the huntress Margo; instead, it is with Wilson. Hemingway admired men who were outsiders, who defied conventional morality and the so-called rules of society. Wilson makes his own rules: If he illegally lashes the natives, it is not because he's sadistic; he simply knows that they'd rather suffer than lose money. It's a simple exchange. Likewise, if he thinks he can bed a woman (or women) who hires him as a safari guide, he takes a double-wide cot on safari; he's not troubled that Francis knows that he is having sex with Margo. Wilson's code is the survival of the fittest, and initially, Francis Macomber proves that he is not fit—although Hemingway stresses at the beginning of this story that Macomber "looked" fit—tall, well-built, trim and healthy. The irony is unmistakable.

Wilson likewise does not abide by conventional rules for hunting game during safaris. Although there's a law against hunting game from vehicles, Wilson thinks that it's far more exciting and dangerous to chase game at high speed. He wants—and needs—the adrenaline rush of danger. Tracking game on foot is child's play.

Fully aware that he would face legal action were the officials in Nairobi to find out that he hunts from moving vehicles, Wilson defies the odds—until Macomber reveals how dangerous a "hunter" his wife, Margot, is: "Now she [Margot] has something on you." This revelation is important, because Margot knows that Macomber is a coward, and she also knows that Wilson is a flagrant lawbreaker. Were this a game of poker, she'd hold the winning hand. Thus Wilson knows that, somehow, he must regain the upper hand over Margo.

Wilson's attitude toward Francis Macomber fluctuates. When Macomber wants to leave the wounded lion, Wilson tells him that "it isn't done." Macomber has no personal code; he *reacts* rather than *acts*. Wilson is perplexed about Macomber's passive/aggressive behavior around his wife, but gaining dominance over Margot is exciting because she seems purposely cruel.

Wilson's flaw is his inability to perceive the psychological state of mind of his clients. In contrast, readers are absolutely aware that Macomber is extremely upset about displaying his cowardice; it began in the night, when he awoke and heard the old lion roaring and then couldn't get back to sleep. He was "afraid . . . [and] there was no one to tell he was afraid." Next morning, Margot recognizes that Macomber is upset, but he tells her simply that he's nervous because of the lion's roaring throughout the night.

Later, after Macomber wounds a lion, his innocence is pitted against the knowledge, experience, and codified values of Wilson. When Macomber discovers that they will have to confront the wounded lion, which is extremely dangerous, Macomber offers all kinds of excuses for not participating in the hunt. First he wonders if they can set the grass afire, but it is too green; then he suggests sending in the beaters, but Wilson says that suggestion is "just a touch murderous." Then Macomber suggests the gun-bearers, and Wilson points out that they have to go in—it's their duty; but he also adds that the beaters "don't look too happy." Significantly, he notices that Macomber is "trembling . . . [with] a pitiful look on his face."

As a last resort, Macomber suggests that they just leave the lion alone, and again Wilson tells him, "It isn't done." When the lion does attack, Macomber, in panic, bolts and runs for the river while the others kill the lion and look at Macomber with contempt. Thus Macomber's cowardice in this scene is the central motivating force for the entire story.

On the way back to camp, Macomber is immediately relegated to the back seat of the motor car even though, on the way out to the bush, he had occupied the front seat. Hemingway is very careful with these details so that he can fully explore the depths to which Macomber has sunk.

Making his embarrassed cowardice even more painful, Macomber watches as Margot reaches forward and puts her hand on Wilson's shoulder, then kisses him on the mouth, calling him "the beautiful red-faced Mr. Wilson." Margot dominates Macomber in this scene, revealing Macomber's enormous cowardice and defeat. The fact that he cannot control his wife's behavior foreshadows what will happen that night when Margot leaves their tent to go to Wilson's tent for the night.

After Margot returns from having sex with Wilson, readers learn about the basis for her marriage to Francis. She is too beautiful for Francis to divorce her, and Francis has too much money for her to ever leave him. Francis confronts her when she returns to their tent, calling her a bitch. She says simply, "Well, you're a coward."

When Macomber reminds Margot that there "wasn't to be any of that. You promised there wouldn't be," we realize that this infidelity has been going on for a long time. Earlier, in years past, Macomber had learned to live with his wife's infidelity, but here, on safari, Margo's sexual betrayal is so open and performed in such defiance because she wants Macomber to know how very much his cowardice has changed everything. And Margot will continue to press her advantage until the end—when she realizes that Macomber is gaining courage and a strong sense of his own manhood.

Much of the genius and brilliance of this story is seen in its careful, technical structuring. The scene that focuses on the shooting and wounding of the lion and Macomber's "bolting like a coward" is paralleled with the scene of the shooting and wounding of the water buffalo. In both cases, Wilson and Macomber and the gunbearers are expected to go in and finish off the wounded animal. In the first scene, Macomber bolts; in the second, he stands his ground and proves his courage.

At first, Margo is ashamed of her husband and uses his cowardice to control and intimidate him; she uses her new-gained control over him to justify her having sex with Wilson and also to remind Macomber that he is a coward. She taunts him in other ways as well; for example, when Macomber says of Wilson, "I hate that red-faced swine. . . . I loathe the sight of him," Margot snidely replies, "He's really very nice." Macomber's dislike stems from the fact that after he asked Wilson if he slept well, Wilson's answer—"Topping!"—infuriates Macomber.

In the last part of the story, an enormous metamorphosis occurs within Macomber, and also within Margot. Seeing the water buffalo, Macomber shoots and Wilson congratulates him on his fine shooting: "You shot damn well." This scene marks the beginning of the tremendous change in Macomber, and he himself feels it happen. In all of his life, he has never felt so good. In contrast, Margot sits "very white faced." She recognizes that Macomber is changing, and she fears this change.

When it's discovered that the first bull water buffalo limped into the bush, Margot is elated, believing that it's going to burst out "just like the lion" and anticipating that Macomber will again "bolt." Wilson, however, has also noticed the change in Macomber and tells Margot that what's going to happen won't "be a damned bit like the lion."

Macomber himself, in truth, had expected the fear to return when the buffalo retreated into the bush, but instead, he realizes that for the first time in his life, he is wholly without fear. Instead of fear, he has a feeling of elation. Even Wilson acknowledges that the day before, Macomber was scared sick, but not anymore; now he is a "ruddy fire eater."

It is Margo who is ill; scared sick, as it were. Whereas she loved the lion hunt, here we have the same situation, but now Macomber finds it marvelous, and it is Margo who screams, "I hate it." Earlier she had looked forward to this hunt because she assumed that Macomber would show his cowardice again. Now she hates it because she realizes that she's losing psychological control over Macomber. Although Margot's marriage to Macomber is based on money, she values her psychological control and power over Macomber as much as she values his money. She certainly knows that if Macomber realizes his strong sense of manhood finally, he will have the strength and courage to leave her—and go hunting for other, younger beauties, because although the story explicitly states that she is still beautiful, she is not as beautiful as she once was.

By now, Wilson fully sympathizes with Macomber. When Macomber says that he will never be afraid of anything again, he tells Wilson that something happened after they first saw the buffalo. It was, he says, "like a dam bursting . . . pure excitement." Wilson realizes that Macomber has definitely undergone a change; he has watched grown men "come of age" in the plains of Africa before.

Macomber has passed and excelled at his initiation into manhood, into the world of courage. And Margo is afraid, "very afraid of something." She tries to taunt him, but he ignores her and becomes almost oblivious to her existence. She now knows that he has found his sense of manhood and that his future does not include her because *he* can change, and perhaps she cannot.

The short, happy life of Francis Macomber begins with his standing solid and shooting for the water buffalo's nose and the heavy horns, "splintering and chipping them"—and then he himself is killed—killed by Margot. His short, happy life lasts for only a second or two, but he dies as master of his own life.

Wilson believes that Margot intentionally shoots her husband, and he makes it quite clear that he knows, boasting that had he lived, Macomber would have left her. He even taunts her with "Why didn't you poison him? That's what they do in England."

One question remains: Because Wilson had become excited about Macomber's new sense of manhood, why does he now seem willing to forget all about her murdering Macomber?

We must remember that Wilson, although he has his own strict code of behavior for safaris and hunting and for his personal conduct, does *not* adhere to the laws of society. He whips natives, he allows clients to shoot from fast-moving vehicles, and he beds clients' wives. If he were to report that the death of Macomber was not an accident, there would have to be an extensive investigation in which all sorts of hunting code violations would be open for investigation, and Wilson could very possibly lose his license.

After all, as Macomber noted earlier, Margot has "something" on Wilson; he knows that he flagrantly disregards laws concerning safari hunts. Thus Wilson has reason to fear Margot, and the only way he can checkmate her is to have "something" on her—her killing of Macomber.

Of all of Hemingway's short stories, this one captures Hemingway's genius for combining exciting subject matter (the great game hunt) with death. Additionally, he has written an initiation story about a man who had never had his courage tested and who had never discovered a sense of manhood until he was thirty-five years old. The story is brilliantly narrated and filled with many ironies and parallels. It not only ranks with the very best of Hemingway's short stories but also with the best American short stories ever written.

- **gimlet**   A popular British colonial drink made from gin and lime juice. Originally it was believed that gimlets were good for staving off scurvy. Since then it has become a popular American drink and is often made with vodka and lime juice.

- **quid**   Slang for the British pound, a currency that—at the time of this story—was worth approximately five dollars.

- **court games**   Squash, handball, and other games played in exclusive men's clubs.

- **giant killer**   liquor; in this case, Scotch whiskey.

- **Swahili**   the so-called "lingua franca," or universal language used through South Central Africa—Kenya, Zaire, Tanzania, Zanzibar, and along the trading coast. Swahili is a mixture of native dialects (principally Bantu) with some Hindi, German, French and English added to it.

- **Mathiaga Club**   A big game hunters club in Nairobi, Kenya. White hunters are professional hunters/guides who arrange and accompany clients on big game hunts, or safaris.

- **buffalo**   The buffalo mentioned in this story is nothing like the American buffalo, or bison. The Cape Buffalo is a large, horned creature that is considered by hunters to be the most dangerous of all African big game. It is mean and cunning and extremely strong, invulnerable to all but the best-placed shots.

- **impala**   A type of antelope that makes prodigious leaps to see if enemies are near. It is very similar to the eland antelope.

- **kippers and coffee** The British are fond of kippered herring—brine-soaked and smoked filets of fish, served most often for breakfast.

- **.505 Gibbs** A very large caliber hunting rifle. While his clients may use smaller guns, a safari guide must carry a sure killer in case the amateur misses and he must make the kill at the last moment—as in the case of Macomber and the lion.

- **gut shot** a shot into the stomach of an animal.

- **Memsahib** "Lady" in Swahili; a title of respect derived from a Hindu word.

- **Bwana** "Mister" or "Master"; a term of respect.

- **windy** British slang for "nervous."

- **Martin Johnson** An American hunter and motion picture producer who made many films about big game hunts.

- **mosquito bar** a net on a bar hung over a cot to keep out insects, particularly mosquitoes.

- **beggar** The word Hemingway originally used was "bugger," a derogatory British term for someone or something disagreeable; however, the term is also synonymous with a sodomite, which was distasteful to Hemingway's editor—thus his substitution of "beggar." Remember that this story was originally published in 1936; today, in the United States, we casually use the term "bastard" with the same non-literal frequency.

- **Mannlicher** an expensive German hunting rifle.

- **wireless** British for "radio."

"HILLS LIKE WHITE ELEPHANTS"

Summary

In the early 1920s, an American man and a girl, probably nineteen or twenty years old, are waiting at a Spanish railway station for the express train that will take them to Madrid. They drink beer as well as two licorice-tasting anis drinks, and finally more beer, sitting in the hot shade and discussing what the American man says will be "a simple operation" for the girl.

The tension between the two is almost as sizzling as the heat of the Spanish sun. The man, while urging the girl to have the operation, says again and again that he really doesn't want her to do it if she really doesn't want to. However, he clearly is insisting that she do so. The girl is trying to be brave and nonchalant but is clearly frightened of committing herself to having the operation. She tosses out a conversational, fanciful figure of speech—noting that the hills beyond the train station "look like white elephants"—hoping that the figure of speech will please the man, but he resents her ploy. He insists on talking even more about the operation and the fact that, according to what he's heard, it's "natural" and "not really an operation at all."

Finally, the express train arrives and the two prepare to board. The girl tells the man that she's "fine." She's lying, acquiescing to what he wants, hoping to quiet him. Nothing has been solved. The tension remains, coiled and tight, as they prepare to leave for Madrid. The girl is hurt by the man's fraudulent, patronizing empathy, and she is also deeply apprehensive about the operation that she will undergo in Madrid.

Commentary

This story was rejected by early editors and was ignored by anthologists until recently. The early editors returned it because they thought that it was a "sketch" or an "anecdote," not a short story. At the time, editors tried to second-guess what the reading public wanted, and, first, they felt as though they had to buy stories that told stories, that had plots. "Hills Like White Elephants" does not tell a story in a traditional manner, and it has no plot.

In part, some of the early rejection of this story lies in the fact that none of the editors who read it had any idea what was going on in the story. Even today, most readers are still puzzled by the story. In other words, it will take an exceptionally perceptive reader to realize immediately that the couple is arguing about the girl's having an abortion at a time when abortions were absolutely illegal, considered immoral, and usually dangerous.

Early objections to this story also cited the fact that there are no traditional characterizations. The female is referred to simply as "the girl," and the male is simply called "the man." There are no physical descriptions of either person or even of their clothing. Unlike traditional stories, wherein the author usually gives us some clues about what the main characters look like, sound like, or dress like, here we know nothing about "the man" or "the girl." We know nothing about their backgrounds. Can we, however, assume something about them—for example, is "the man" somewhat older and "the girl" perhaps younger, maybe eighteen or nineteen? One reason for assuming this bare-bones guesswork lies in tone of "the girl." Her questions are not those of a mature, worldly-wise woman, but, instead, they are those of a young person who is eager and anxious to please the man she is with.

It is a wonder that this story was published at all. When it was written, authors were expected to guide readers through a story. In "Hills Like White Elephants," though, Hemingway completely removes himself from the story. Readers are never aware of an author's voice behind the story. Compare this narrative technique to the traditional nineteenth-century method of telling a story. Then, such authors as Dickens or Trollope would often address their readers directly.

In contrast, we have no idea how to react to Hemingway's characters. Had Hemingway said that the girl, for example, spoke "sarcastically," or "bitterly," or "angrily," or that she was "puzzled" or "indifferent," or if we were told that the man spoke with "an air of superiority," we could more easily come to terms with these characters. Instead, Hemingway so removes himself from them and their actions that it seems as though he himself knows little about them. Only by sheer accident, it seems, is the girl nick-named "Jig."

That said, during the latter part of the 1990s, this story has become one of the most anthologized of Hemingway's short stories. In part, this new appreciation for the story lies in Hemingway's use of dialogue to convey the "meaning" of the story—that is, there is no description, no narration, no identification of character or intent. We have no clear ideas about the nature of the discussion (abortion), and yet the dialogue does convey everything that we conclude about the characters.

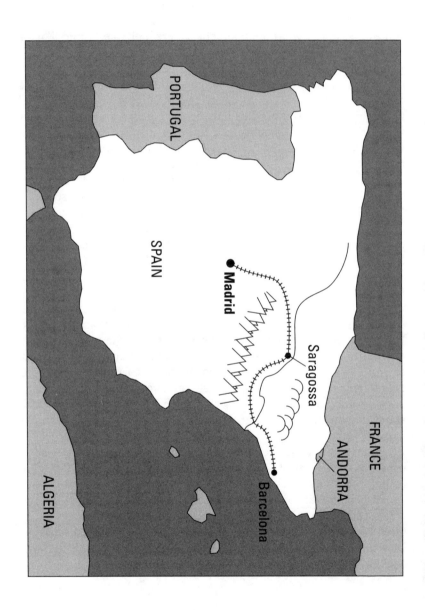

Map Explanation

"Hills Like White Elephants" is set in Spain. An American man and a girl are sitting at an outdoor café in a Spanish train station, waiting for a fast, non-stop train coming from Barcelona that will take them to Madrid, where the girl will have an abortion.

In the story, Hemingway refers to the Ebro River and to the bare, sterile-looking mountains on one side of the train station and to the fertile plains on the other side of the train station. The hills of Spain, to the girl, are like white elephants in their bareness and round, protruding shape. Also notable is that "white elephant" is a term used to refer to something that requires much care and yielding little profit; an object no longer of any value to its owner but of value to others; and something of little or no value. Throughout this dialogue, the girl's crumbling realization that she is not truly loved is a strong undercurrent that creates tension and suppressed fear.

"A Clean, Well-Lighted Place" takes place in Spain as well. It centers around two waiters and an elderly man who patronizes the café late at night before closing time. He is a drunk who has just tried to kill himself. One of the waiters is older and understands the elderly man's loneliness and how important the café is to the old man's mental health.

Hemingway explores older men's loneliness by using the older waiter as a sounding board for the elderly man's defense. Although the elderly man is without a companion or anyone waiting at home for him, he indulges his lapses from reality in a dignified and refined manner, expressed in his choosing of a clean, well-lighted place in the late hours of the night. The importance of the clean, well-lighted place where one can sit is integral to maintaining dignity and formality amidst loneliness, despair and desperation.

In addition, the popularity of this story can be found in the change in readers' expectations. Readers in the 1990s had become accustomed to reading between the lines of fictional narrative and didn't like to be told, in minute detail, everything about the characters. They liked the fact that Hemingway doesn't even say whether or not the two characters are married. He presents only the conversation between them and allows his readers to draw their own conclusions. Thus readers probably assume that these two people are not married; however, if we are interested enough to speculate about them, we must ask ourselves how marriage would affect their lives. And to answer this question, we must make note of one of the few details in the story: their luggage. Their luggage has "labels on them from all the hotels where they had spent nights." Were these two people, the man and the girl, to have this child, their incessant wanderings might have to cease and they would probably have to begin a new lifestyle for themselves; additionally, they might have to make a decision whether or not they should marry and legitimize the child. Given their seemingly free style of living and their relish for freedom, a baby and a marriage would impose great changes in their lives.

Everything in the story indicates that the man definitely wants the girl to have an abortion. Even when the man maintains that he wants the girl to have an abortion *only* if *she* wants to have one, we question his sincerity and his honesty. When he says, "If you don't want to you don't have to. I wouldn't have you do it if you didn't want to," he is not convincing. From his earlier statements, it is obvious that he does *not* want the responsibility that a child would entail; seemingly, he strongly wants her to have this abortion and definitely seems to be very unresponsive to the girl's feelings.

On the other hand, we feel that the girl is not at all sure that she wants an abortion. She's ambivalent about the choice. We sense that she is tired of traveling, of letting the man make all the decisions, of allowing the man to talk incessantly until he convinces her that *his* way is the *right* way. He has become her guide and her guardian. He translates for her, even now: Abortion involves only a doctor allowing "a little air in." Afterward, they will be off on new travels. However, for the girl, this life of being ever in flux, living in hotels, traveling, and never settling down has become wearying. Their life of transience, of instability, is described by the girl as living on the surface: "[We] look at things and try new drinks."

When the man promises to be with the girl during the "simple" operation, we again realize his insincerity because what is "simple" to him may very well be emotionally and physically damaging to her.

The man is using *his* logic in order to be as persuasive as possible. Without a baby anchoring them down, they can continue to travel; they can "have everything." However, the girl contradicts him and, at that moment, seems suddenly strong and more in control of the situation. With or without the abortion, things will never be the same. She also realizes that she is not loved, at least not unconditionally.

Thus we come to the title of the story. The girl has looked at the mountains and has said that they look "like white elephants." Immediately, a tension between the two mounts until the man says, "Oh, cut it out." She maintains that he started the argument, then she slips into apology, stating that, of course, the mountains don't really look like white elephants—only "their skin through the trees."

From the man's point of view, the hills don't look like white elephants, and the hills certainly don't have skins. The girl, however, has moved away from the rational world of the man and into her own world of intuition, in which she seemingly knows that the things that she desires will never be fulfilled. This insight is best illustrated when she looks across the river and sees fields of fertile grain and the river—the fertility of the land, contrasted to the barren sterility of the hills like white elephants. She, of course, desires the beauty, loveliness, and fertility of the fields of grain, but she knows that she has to be content with the barren sterility of an imminent abortion and the continued presence of a man who is inadequate. What she will ultimately do is beyond the scope of the story.

During the very short exchanges between the man and the girl, she changes from someone who is almost completely dependent upon the man to someone who is more sure of herself and more aware of what to expect from him. At the end of their conversation, she takes control of herself and of the situation: She no longer acts in her former childlike way. She tells the man to please shut up—and note that the word "please" is repeated seven times, indicating that she is overwhelmingly tired of his hypocrisy and his continual harping on the same subject.

- **the Ebro** a river in northeastern Spain; the second longest river in Spain.
- **the express** a direct, non-stop train.
- **white elephant** something of little or no value.

"A CLEAN, WELL-LIGHTED PLACE"

Summary

Late in the early morning hours, in a Spanish cafe, an old man drinks brandy. A young waiter is angry; he wishes that the old man would leave so that he and an older waiter could close the cafe and go home. He insults the deaf old man and is painfully indifferent to the older waiter's feelings when he states that "an old man is a nasty thing." The older waiter, however, realizes that the old man drinking brandy after brandy is not nasty; he is only lonely. No doubt, that's the reason why the old man tried to hang himself last week.

When the old man leaves, the waiters close the cafe. The young waiter leaves for home, and the older waiter walks to an all-night cafe where, thinking about the terrible emptiness of the old man's life which he keenly identifies with, he orders a cup of *nada* from the waiter. A cup of nothing. The man who takes the order thinks that the old waiter is just another crazy old man; he brings him coffee.

Finishing the coffee, the older waiter begins his trudge homeward. Sleep is hours away. Until then, he must try to cope bravely with the dark nothingness of the night.

Commentary

What happens in this story? Nothing. What do the characters stand for? Nothing. What is the plot? Nothing. In fact, because there is no plot, Hemingway enables us to focus absolutely on the story's meaning—that is, in a world characterized by nothingness, what possible action *could* take place? Likewise, that no character has a name and that there is no characterization emphasize the sterility of this world.

What then is the theme of this story? Nothing, or nothingness. This is exactly what the story is about: nothingness and the steps we take against it. When confronting a world that is meaningless, how is someone who has rejected all of the old values, someone who is now completely alone—how is that person supposed to face this barren world? How is that person able to avoid the darkness of *nada*, or nothingness?

The setting is a clean Spanish cafe, where two unnamed waiters—one old and one young—are discussing an old man (also unnamed) who comes every night, sits alone, and drinks brandy until past closing time. The young waiter mentions that the old man tried to commit suicide last week. When the old waiter asks why the old man tried to commit suicide, the young waiter tells him that the old man was consumed by despair. "Why?" asks the old waiter. "Nothing," answers the young waiter.

The young waiter reveals that there is absolutely no reason to commit suicide if one has money—which he's heard the old man has. For the young waiter, money solves all problems. For an old, rich man to try to commit suicide over the despair of confronting nothingness is beyond the young waiter's understanding. However, nothingness is the reason that the old man comes to the cafe every night and drinks until he is drunk.

In contrast, the old waiter knows all about despair, for he remains for some time after the lights have gone off at the clean, earlier well-lighted cafe. The old waiter also knows fear. "It was not fear or dread," Hemingway says of the old waiter, "it was a nothing that he knew too well. It was a nothing and a man was nothing too." After stopping for a drink at a cheap, all-night bar, the old waiter knows that he will not sleep until morning, when it is light.

The story emphasizes lateness—late not only in terms of the hour of the morning (it's almost 3 A.M.), but also in terms of the old man's and the old waiter's lives. Most important, however, is the emphasis on religious traditions—specifically, on the Spanish Catholic tradition, because faith in the promises of Catholicism can no longer support or console these old men. Thus, suicide is inviting.

The old man who drinks brandy at the clean, well-lighted cafe is literally deaf, just as he is metaphorically deaf to the outmoded traditions of Christianity and Christian promises: He cannot hear them any more. He is alone, he is isolated, sitting in the shadow left by nature in the modern, artificial world. Additionally, all of the light remaining is artificial light—in this clean, "well-lighted" cafe.

What is important in the story is not only the condition of nothingness in the world but the way that the old man and the old waiter feel and respond to this nothingness. Thus, Hemingway's real subject matter is the feeling of man's condition of nothingness—and not the nothingness itself. Note, though, that neither of the old men is a passive victim. The old man has his dignity. And when the young waiter says that old men are nasty, the old waiter does not deny the general truth of this statement, but he does come to the defense of the old man by pointing out that this particular old man is clean and that he likes to drink brandy in a clean, well-lighted place. And the old man *does* leave with dignity. This is not much—this aged scrap of human dignity—in the face of the human condition of nothingness, but, Hemingway is saying, sometimes it is all that we have.

The young waiter wants the old man to go to one of the all-night cafes, but the old waiter objects because he believes in the importance of cleanliness and light. Here, in this well-lighted cafe, the light is a manmade symbol of man's attempt to hold off the darkness—not permanently, but as late as possible. The old man's essential loneliness is less intolerable in light, where there is dignity. The danger of being alone, in darkness, in nothingness, is suicide.

At this point, we can clearly see differences between the old waiter and the young waiter—especially in their antithetical attitudes toward the old man. Initially, however, the comments of both waiters concerning a passing soldier and a young girl seem very much alike; they both seem to be cynical. Yet when the young waiter says of the old man, "I wouldn't want to be that old. An old man is a nasty thing," then we see a clear difference between the two waiters because the old waiter defends the old man: "This old man is clean. He drinks without spilling. Even now, drunk."

The young waiter refuses to serve the old man another drink because he wants to get home to his wife, and, in contrast, the old waiter is resentful of the young waiter's behavior. The old waiter knows what it is like to have to go home in the dark; he himself will not go home to sleep until daybreak—when he will not have to fall asleep in the nothingness of darkness.

Thus, in a sense, the old waiter is partially Hemingway's spokesperson because he points out that the old man leaves the cafe walking with dignity; he affirms the cleanliness of the old man. Unlike the young waiter, who is impetuous and has a wife to go home to, the old waiter is unhurried because he has no one waiting for him; he has no place to go except to his empty room. The old waiter is wiser, more tolerant, and more sensitive than the young waiter.

What Hemingway is saying is this: In order to hold nothingness, darkness, *nada* at bay, we must have light, cleanliness, order (or discipline), and dignity. If everything else has failed, man must have something to resort to or else the only option is suicide—and that is the ultimate end of everything: "It is all nothing that he knew too well. It was all nothing and a man was nothing. It was only that and light . . . and a certain cleanness and order."

At the end of the story, the old waiter is alone in a cheap bar, a "bodega," which is well-lighted—but not clean. Because he has been contemplating the concept of *nada*, he says, when the barman asks for his order, "*Nada*," which prompts the barman to tell him (in Spanish) that he's crazy. Realizing the truth of what he has heard, the old waiter responds with the now-well-known parody of the Lord's Prayer: "Our nada who art in nada . . ."

Left alone, the old waiter is isolated with his knowledge that all is nothing. He is standing at a dirty, unpolished bar. He cannot achieve even the dignity that the old man at the cafe possessed; he also knows that he will not sleep. Perhaps he has amnesia, but we know better: The old waiter cannot sleep because he is afraid of the darkness, afraid of nothingness. Hemingway himself suffered severe bouts of insomnia, feeling alone and deserted in the universe.

- **pesata** a coin of small value.

- **hombre** man

- **bodegas** cafes serving alcoholic beverages.

"THE SNOWS OF KILIMANJARO"

Summary

Harry, a writer, and his wife, Helen, are stranded while on safari in Africa. A bearing burned out on their truck, and Harry is talking about the gangrene that has infected his leg when he did not apply iodine after he scratched it. As they wait for a rescue plane from Nairobi that he knows won't arrive on time, Harry spends his time drinking and insulting Helen. Harry reviews his life, realizing that he wasted his talent through procrastination and luxury from a marriage to a wealthy woman that he doesn't love.

In a series of flashbacks, Harry recalls the mountains of Bulgariaand Constantinople, as well as the suddenly hollow, sick feeling of being alone in Paris. Later, there were Turks, and an American poet talking nonsense about the Dada movement, and headaches and quarrels, and watching people whom he would later write about. Uneasily, he recalls a boy who'd been frozen, his body half-eaten by dogs, and a wounded officer so entangled in a wire fence that his bowels spilled over it.

As Harry lies on his cot, he is aware that vultures are walking around his makeshift camp, and a hyena lurks in the shadows. Knowing that he will die before he wakes, Harry goes to sleep and dreams that the rescue plane is taking him to a snow covered summit of Kilimanjaro, the highest mountain in Africa. Its Western summit is called the Masai "Ngàje Ngài," the House of God, where he sees the legendary leopard.

Helen wakes, and taking a flashlight, walks toward Harry's cot. Seeing that his leg is dangling alongside the cot and that the dressings are pulled down, she calls his name repeatedly. She listens for his breathing and can hear nothing. Outside the tent, the hyena whines—a cry that is strangely human.

Commentary

Hemingway opens his story with an epigraph, a short, pithy observation about a lone leopard who sought the tip of Kilimanjaro (literally, "The House of God").

The African safari was Harry's attempt to put his life back on track. Harry, the central character, has been living a life of sloth, luxury, and procrastination, so this safari was supposed to bring him back to the virtues of hard work, honesty, and struggle as a step in the right direction. Living off of his wife's wealth has led him down a path of steady, artistic decline and he knows it.

Also interesting to note is that both Harry and Hemingway were of the "Lost Generation" of World War I who had to rebuild their lives after being wounded in combat and seeing the horrors of war. This particular work, some have asserted, seems to reflect both Harry's and Hemingway's concerns about leaving unfinished business behind as a writer and the proper lifestyle for a writer that is conducive to writing on a daily basis. Hemingway was quoted as saying once that "politics, women, drink, money, and ambition" ruin writers.

Concerning the structure of this story, note that Hemingway divides it into six sections and within each of these sections inserts a flashback that appears in italic, continually juxtaposing the hopeless, harrowing present with the past, which often seemed full of promise.

The flashbacks themselves center around concerns about the erosion of values: lost love, loose sex, drinking, revenge, and war. They are a mix of hedonism, sentimentality toward the human condition, and leaving unfinished business. Here, in this story, the symbolism of Kilimanjaro is contrasted with the symbolism of the plains. Harry is dying in the plains from gangrene, a stinking, putrid, and deadly infection, causing his body to rot and turn greenish black. Against Harry's background of dark, smelly horror and hopelessness, Hemingway contrasts Harry's memories of the good times that he had in the mountains. Good things happen in the mountains; bad things happen on the plains. Hemingway ends his story with Harry's spirit triumphant, as when Harry dies, his spirit is released and travels to the summit of the mighty mountain where the square top of Kilimanjaro is "wide as all the world"; it is incredibly white as it shines dazzlingly in the sunlight. The mountain is brilliant, covered with pure white snow; it is incredibly clean—a clean, well-lighted place.

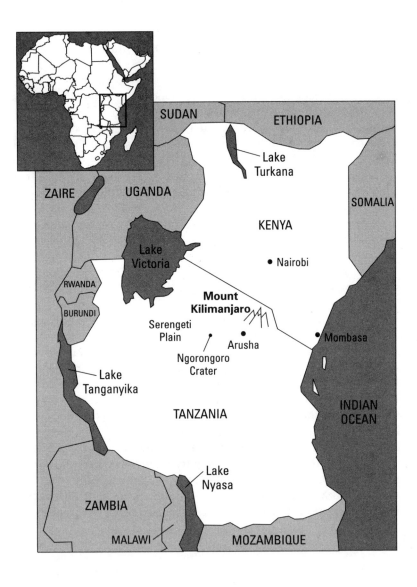

Map Explanation

The setting for Hemingway's "The Short Happy Life of Francis Macomber" is Africa. Robert Wilson, the Macombers' safari guide, has sex with Margo Macomber; afterward, when Wilson chides Francis about his cowardice and Margo's mocking behavior toward Francis, Francis reminds Wilson that Margo is aware that if the authorities in Nairobi knew about Wilson's less-than-professional hunting of wild animals, he could lose his license. Both Francis and Wilson have secrets that Margo can blackmail them with. Thus Margo becomes a hunter and corners both her husband and Wilson.

Hemingway also uses Africa as the setting for "Snows of Kilimanjaro," in which an American writer and his wife are waiting for a plane to fly the dying writer to a hospital. As he is dying, Harry imagines that he is aboard the plane and that he can see the square-topped summit of Kilimanjaro—perpetually snow-covered, mysterious, and pure.

It is important to note here that there were three deeds throughout Harry's life that facilitated his otherworldly trip to Kilimanjaro at the time of this death:

- Giving away his last morphine pills that he saved for himself to his friend Williamson, who is in horrendous pain
- Harry's intention to write (the mental writing of the flashbacks) in his painful stupor
- Sacrificing himself to his wife as opposed to absolving himself

During his otherworldly flight over Kilimanjaro, Harry sees the legendary leopard. The dead, preserved leopard can be seen as a symbol of immortality, a reward for taking the difficult road. Harry himself was a "leopard" at certain times in his life, as were some of his acquaintances in his own stories. Specifically, Harry can be seen as a leopard during

- His youth, when he lived in a poor neighborhood of Paris as a writer
- In the war, when he gave his last morphine pills for himself to the horribly suffering Williamson
- On his deathbed, when he mentally composes flashbacks and uses his intention to write
- When he stays loyal to his wife and does not confess to her that he never really loved her

Some mystic impulse within Harry and within the leopard drove them to seek out God, or the god within themselves, or immortality that resided far from ugly, mundane reality.

In most civilizations, God or God's promise of immortality resides on the highest mountain top: Mount Olympus for the Greeks, Mount Sinai for the Hebrews, Mount Fuji for the Japanese. If the leopard was searching for some sort of immortality, then it found immortality at the summit of Kilimanjaro, where it lies frozen—preserved for all eternity.

When Harry looks at Kilimanjaro, he sees it as a symbol of truth, idealism, and purity. When he dies, tragic irony exists. The leopard died in a high, clean, well-lighted place; Harry, in contrast, dies rotting and stinking on the plains, lamenting his wasted life and his failure to complete his desired projects.

In his novels and especially in his short stories, Hemingway often uses mountains to symbolize goodness, the purity, and cleanness, and he uses the plains as a symbol of evil and confusion. This contrast has often been commented on by Hemingway scholars.

Not surprisingly, because death is at the core of this story, one of the central themes that occurs again and again in Hemingway's stories and novels is man's direct encounter with death or with approaching death. Whether a man is in war and on the battlefield (as Nick Adams is in several stories; as are Hemingway heroes in his novels *A Farewell to Arms, For Whom the Bell Tolls*, and parts of *The Sun Also Rises*) or facing death (as Nick Adams is when he is severely wounded in "A Way You'll Never Be" and "In Another Country"), or on big game hunts, facing charging animals (as Francis Macomber is in "A Short Happy Life"), the theme of man's direct encounter with death is always pivotal to the story. Death is always present as Hemingway examines how man reacts and behaves in the face of death. In this case, as with other of Hemingway's heroes, we have a writer, Harry, who never writes what he has wanted to; now it is too late. Death is so near that it can be smelled, even in the presence of the stinking, smelly hyena.

PART 1

Hemingway opens this story with a typical Hemingway narrative device: Two people are talking; moreover, they are talking about pain and a horrible odor. Hemingway zeroes in on the immediate problem: Harry's certain death—unless help arrives. Hemingway does not immediately identify the people who are talking; and readers don't yet know the names of the characters, the place, the time, or any other kind of background, expository information about them. Readers know only that something is terribly wrong with the male character, causing a potent stench, and that three big birds squat "obscenely" close by. The woman's first comment—"Don't! Please don't."—indicates that tension exists between her and the man, a tension that will soon erupt into antagonism.

Also, mainly through conversation only, readers learn that the man has some type of injury but that the pain has disappeared; he is lying on a cot under some trees while "obscene" birds (vultures) are circling overhead. A truck that the man and woman were driving has broken down, and they are now waiting for a rescue plane to take them away.

The man mentions for the first time that the big birds—the vultures (or buzzards, as they are often referred to)—are birds of prey, who have ceased circling over Harry and Helen and now have begun to walk around on the ground. They seemingly *know* that Harry is close to death. During the day, the ugly vultures gather around the camp; the putrid, foul smell of Harry's rotting, gangrenous flesh attracts them. Hemingway uses the symbol of the vulture in its natural setting, Africa, to convey the horror of approaching death and the agony of waiting for death. Ironically, the reader also learns that in happier times, Harry spent time observing the vulture's behavior so that he could use them in his writing.

As spiritual symbols of ascension, these birds represent both what could've been and what now can't be. It is interesting to note that Hemingway chose the vulture to represent Harry's "cycle" of opportunity and termination, as vultures themselves are inherently tied to global life and death on the plain because of their ecological function. Life, because their scavenging enables the plain to stay clean and free of rotten debris that could be harmful to other animals, and death, because they portend when an animal will expire and become carrion. In essence, these "trash men" of the plains are also the trash men of Harry's wasted life. They appeared at a time when Harry could have cleaned up his lifestyle and used his ability when he had his health, and now they appear again as Harry is about to die. These vultures represent Harry's physical death. Vultures have long been a symbol of death and rebirth in American Indian folklore as well.

The woman mentions that she would like to do something for Harry until the rescue plane arrives. The plane, of course, is another symbol. The airplane is airborne—that is, from the heavens—it is a symbol that is filled with hope that Harry and Helen can escape from the plains and from the horrible vultures.

This is the beginning of the jarring realization that Harry has run out of time and that all of the writing he planned to do will never get done. Camping on the hot, sweltering plain at the foot of Kilimanjaro, Harry vents his anger and frustration at himself onto his wife. It is on this low, hot plain with land-bound animals that Harry is at his most frustrated, baser, unrealized self as death, symbolized by the vultures, creeps nearer and his unused talent slips further away from him.

Harry's impending death causes him to evaluate his life. He knows now that he will never "write the things that he had saved to write until he knew enough to write them well." Now it is too late, and he will never know "if he could have written them." His day-by-day closing in on death makes him realize how often and how much he frittered away his life, avoiding writing the things that he wanted to. Thus, Hemingway combines two themes: man's confrontation with death and man as a failed artist.

FLASHBACK 1

All of the five flashbacks (some literary critics refer to them as "interior monologues") deal with brief scenes, or vignettes, about the things that Harry experienced in the past; he had meant to write about them but never did.

In this first flashback, snow is a central element in each of his recollections. He remembers the railway station in Karagatch, Turkey, and leaving on the famous Orient Express and riding through northern Greece, where he recalled fighting between the Greeks and Turks (during the Greco-Turko war that Hemingway, when he was a reporter, covered).

He remembers Bulgaria: the mountains covered with snow; the exchange of populations and people walking in the snow until they died in it. There, he also protected a deserter. While snowed in at the Madlener-haus for a week, the owner of the gasthaus lost everything while gambling. There in the cold, bright mountains someone named Barker bombed Austrian officers' leave train and strafed those who escaped and then came into the Austrian mess hall and bragged about it.

He remembers Vorarlberg and Arlberg, winter ski resorts with many activities, including skiing on the snow like a bird in the air (Hemingway skied often in these places); Harry never wrote about any of these adventures.

Throughout this section, there is an overwhelming sense of loss. Loss of lives from war, and loss of life due to despair and adverse financial circumstances. Throughout the flashback, the snow sets the stage for spiritual ascension and release. Spiritual ascension in terms of being released during death, although through unpleasant means, from the earthly plane, and release in terms of finding joy and peace in skiing free and unfettered in the wind.

A second level of loss is also the loss of opportunity. All of these experiences in this flashback are ripe opportunities for artistic expression, as they are events that Harry experienced himself and knew. Harry went many places and saw many things, but never wrote about any of them.

PART 2

Here, the narrative is divided into two sections, separated by three asterisks (* * *). The first section of this narrative resumes the conversation between Harry and his wife, but now it becomes more bitter and hateful. When she reminds him that in Paris he loved a place where they stayed, he angrily responds that "Love is a dunghill," which debases their love. She asks him if he must destroy everything by killing his horse and wife and burning his saddle and armor. She alludes to a warrior's trophies that were set afire after the death of a warrior. Harry blames her "bloody money" for his predicament; then he repents and lies to her about his love for her. Lastly, he admits that his abuse stems from frustration about leaving things behind that he never did. It is here that the reader gets the most vivid glance into Harry's bitterness, rage, and frustration at himself and at his wife for what she represents in his life.

In the second section, he later wakens and discovers that Helen is away, hoping to shoot a Tommie (a small gazelle) for meat and broth. The sun has gone down, and although the vultures are no longer walking on the ground around the camp, they are roosting for the night in a nearby tree in greater numbers. Even the stillness and cover of the night and the comfort of sleep do not rid Harry of the feathered reminders of his impending death; even while roosting to sleep, the vultures are ever vigilant of his continuing decline. The small animals scurrying on the ground are another yet minor symbol to note, as they indicate that life still goes on, business as usual, all around Harry despite his life-threatening situation.

Harry considers his procrastination—not writing, and writing becoming daily more and more difficult. Finally, he did no work at all. Almost without knowing it, he traded his artistic talents for money and comfort, and the exchange was not worth it. He acknowledges, however, that it was not his wife's fault. If it had not been Helen, there would have been another rich woman. Also, he realizes that he destroyed his talent for writing by drinking so much that his perceptions were finally blunted.

Helen returns with game—a male Tommie that she successfully shot. As Helen and Harry are having drinks, a hyena appears in the early evening, just it has been doing for two weeks. Hemingway uses the hyena as the second important, prominent symbol of Harry's deterioration. The hyena is another carrion eater that is probably the most despised of all African animals because of its filth and aggressive team efforts to destroy and to steal other animals wounded and suffering on the plain. In this sense, the hyena can represent Harry's loveless marriage and the moral sloth of choosing material comfort over true love, because it is these two elements intermingled in his marriage that are the most destructive to him as a writer. Hence, although the hyena is a symbol of death, it is a spiritual death as opposed to a physical one.

Seeing the hyena, knowing about the vultures, and realizing that his wife and her money all symbolize the death of an artist, Harry suddenly knows for certain that he is actually going to die here on the plains of Africa.

However, even at this point, he realizes that Helen does really love him whether he really loves her, and he sees that she is a good, honest woman. He likes her pleasantness and appreciation and admires her shooting. Instead of having an honest conversation about his real feelings for her, he sacrifices himself to her to avoid hurting her, and chooses not to make any deathbed confessions that would cause her emotional pain. Because he doesn't break with her and stays true to her in the end, he reestablishes his higher self. This is the second one of the three important deeds of his life that facilitates his flight over Kilimanjaro at the end of the story.

Helen is improved by her association with Harry, as he makes her life complete. She has selfless love and respect for him, and is considered to be one of Hemingway's heroic women. Conversely,

Harry has declined because he has lived hypocritically with a woman he doesn't love.

FLASHBACK 2

Harry remembers quarreling in Paris and going to Constantinople and spending his time having sex with all kinds of women and finally getting into fights. After one fight, he decided to leave for Anatolia, the great plains of Turkey, where poppies are grown for opium. He recalls what strange things opium did for him: He seemed to see men wearing white ballet skirts and upturned shoes with pom-poms on their toes. He saw such horrors that when he returned to Paris, he couldn't talk about it or write about it.

In Paris, Harry met Tristian Tzara, a Romanian poet who founded the Dada movement (Dadaism) and who represented everything that Harry (and Hemingway) opposed. Harry "had never written any of this," but he'd like to write about it.

This particular flashback focuses on escapism, futility, and what doesn't come to fruition, particularly in Harry's relationships with women. The empty, one-night sexual encounters with women, winning a fight with a man for a woman he has for one evening, and the sentimental relapse for a past love that ruins his present marriage all are in response to a quarrel that happened and then passed.

Another level of futility can also be seen in the war. Harry and the British observer run as fast as they can, only to see the Turks coming upon them as they hide.

Rather than facing his feelings, Harry escapes into the world of booze, one-night stands, as well as opium for altered states of consciousness that enable him to forget the quarrel with his wife and the war.

PART 3

Harry feels as if he's going to die tonight; he wants to sleep outside. Helen brings him broth to keep up his strength, but he doesn't need any "strength" to die. He wants to write and wonders if Helen can take dictation so that he could record his last thoughts. If he were able to write one perfect paragraph, one last time, he could "get it right." Despite his physical deterioration, Harry still yearns for one last chance and entertains hope that maybe his wife could do the physical aspect of the writing for him.

FLASHBACK 3

Here, this third flashback deals with two themes: destruction and a lingering loss despite recovery and rebuilding; and productivity and happiness in the midst of poverty.

Harry recalls his grandfather's log house that burned and destroyed all of his grandfather's guns, and how even though it was rebuilt, his grandfather never bothered to get more guns and never hunted again. Even though the log house was rebuilt, the remnants of the destroyed guns lay in the ashes of the fire like a coffin in its crypt, with his grandfather and everyone else giving the remnants of the guns the same respect and berth due a gravesite.

He then remembers Germany's Black Forest, where he went after the war and fished; he remembers the hotel where, because of inflation, the proprietor lost all his money and because he didn't have enough money from the previous year to buy supplies and open the hotel, he hanged himself. Although the hotel may have lingered after the inflation, the proprietor was lost forever.

Harry recalls all of the little neighborhoods in Paris where he lived when he was poor, including the drunkards and the sportifs; he remembers the inexpensive hotel where he rented the top room to live in and write. He could see the rooftops of Paris from his window and observe the various things that were happening in the streets below.

Here, these poor little neighborhoods in Paris were full of vivid characters and vital people, productive in some way and happy despite their poverty. It was here that Harry was penniless yet productive, enjoying the people-watching opportunities and quaint beauty that these neighborhoods offered. It was his favorite part of Paris, and it represents his youth, happiness, and potential.

The purple dye that the flower sellers use to dye the flowers could be an interesting metaphor for writing itself. The purple dye could represent the creative license, liberty, and literary devices that writers use to color real life events with to create their fiction.

Important here also is the mention of the famous writer Paul Verlain dying in a cheap hotel in the neighborhood. This talented writer's demise in this neighborhood parallels Harry's potential for talent and demise as well, as Harry's demise started when he left this neighborhood and abandoned this lifestyle.

PART 4

Harry's wife wants him to drink some broth; instead, he asks for whiskey. He waits; after Helen leaves, he'll drink all he wants. He considers sleep, but death seems to have gone down a different street, on a bicycle. Harry is hallucinating, rapidly approaching his death.

FLASHBACK 4

Harry realizes that he never wrote about many things: a ranch and a "half-wit chore boy" who was given the task of protecting the farm in the absence of the owner. When another farmer, a mean-spirited, sadistic man, tried to get himself some feed from the barn and threatened to beat the chore boy if he tried to stop him, the chore boy was loyal to the owner. That was when the chore boy got a rifle, shot the man, and left him for the dogs to eat. Harry remembers taking the carcass into town with the chore boy's help, who thought he was going to be rewarded for protecting his master's property, but to his amazement, was arrested and handcuffed. Then he turned to Harry and began to cry.

That was one story that Harry had "saved to write." He's sure that he has at least twenty good stories inside him, stories that he would never write.

This particular flashback deals with misguided loyalty. Although the chore boy protected the hay and was loyal to the owner as he was told to do, his misguided sense of how to be loyal and protect his owner results in a grisly crime and desecration of a corpse.

PART 5

Looking at his rich wife, Harry gives us his view of the rich and of the very rich. Harry recalls talking about this subject with

Julian. Actually, this same conversation occurred between Hemingway and F. Scott Fitzgerald. Some biographers have placed the conversation in a cafe in Paris, when Fitzgerald told Hemingway, "The very rich are different from you and me." And Hemingway replied, "Yes, they have more money."

Harry is also fighting intense, prolonged pain and is trying to overcome it by not caring about it. Just when he thinks he can't bear it, it goes away.

FLASHBACK 5

Harry remembers the death of a soldier named Williamson, who had been hit by a bomb and, while he was trying to move, realized that he was snagged and caught in a wire fence with his bowels spilling out onto the wire. He begged Harry to kill him. This is the only flashback in this short story where Harry doesn't mention that he failed to write about a certain memory or memories.

This particular flashback was one Harry probably didn't want to write about, as it deals with a man who "couldn't stand things." Readers aren't told whether Williamson could've survived. However, the fact that he was brought from the battlefield alive and conscious for some time even after being given a fatal dose of morphine pills that Harry saved for himself indicated to Harry that Williamson was a very strong man. Despite his strength, he didn't wait to find out whether the Lord gave him more than he could bear. He simply didn't try to beat the pain.

This is the first deed of the three in Harry's life that facilitates his flight to Kilimanjaro. Because Harry sacrifices the morphine pills to ease Williamson's pain, this episode is parallel to the one in Part 2 where Harry sacrifices himself to his wife and stays loyal to her as opposed to absolving himself and admitting that he never loved her.

PART 6

For Harry, death has been easy compared to the soldier who was impaled on the wire fence; in fact, death has become boring for Harry—he's as bored with it as he is with everything else.

Also, he tells his wife that "I've been writing." At this point in the story, Harry's intention is as good as his deed. In his current situation, Harry feels that he has done everything he can (in intention) to redeem himself and be worthy of Heaven before he dies. This is the final of the three deeds that facilitates Harry's eventual flight over Kilimanjaro.

At that moment, he feels "death come by again"—a hyena—resting its head on the foot of his cot.

Harry tells his wife, Helen: "Never believe any of that about a scythe and a skull." These traditional Western-world medieval symbols of death are not valid in Africa. Here, the vulture and the hyena dominate Harry's sure knowledge of his inevitable death. Indeed, the hyena becomes the more dominant symbol when it sits, "pressing," on Harry's chest.

At this point, readers should realize that Harry has died. At the point of death, ideas and dreams are reality for Harry, so the trip to Kilimanjaro (Heaven) is *not* in italic. For Harry, the reality is that the rescue plane has come and he has been saved and rewarded. There are two images of Harry ascending—one, when he is lifted from the cot to take him inside, and the other, when the plane lifts off and heads toward Mount Kilimanjaro. For some readers, there are more endings than simply this one. One occurs when the hyena presses on Harry's chest, signifying his death. The other ending occurs when the plane flies Harry toward the square top of Kilimanjaro.

Metaphorically, a few things happen here to indicate that the flight to Kilimanjaro isn't a worldy trip:

- Compton refuses the cup of tea before he and Harry leave
- There is no room in the plane for any passengers except for Harry
- The plane doesn't go to Arusha to refuel

The plane veers toward the white, shining, square top of Kilimanjaro, for, at that moment, Harry knows "where he [is] going."

To summarize, the deeds that Harry does that secure his flight to Kilimanjaro are:

- He gives his morphine pills to Williamson
- Harry's intention to write (the mentally composed flashbacks) in a painful stupor
- He sacrifices himself to his wife by not telling her that he never really loved her to absolve himself

For Harry's wife, the reality is that Harry is dead and she is alone again.

- **odor** Gangrene is literally a putrefaction, emitting a horrible, rotten stench.

- **big birds** here, vultures, carrion eaters attracted to Harry's rotting flesh.

- **Tommies** The reference is to the Thompson's gazelle, a small antelope.

- **Black's** a home remedy medical book.

- **Bwana** Mister, or master; a term of respect.

- **Kikuyu** a member of a Kenya tribe.

- **Karagach** a town in Turkey.

- **Simplon-Orient** Also known as the Orient Express, it was, in its heyday, the most famous and elegant train on any continent.

- **Thrace** A section of Greece, it was the scene of fighting between the Greeks and the Turks in 1922.

- **Nansen** Fridtjof Nansen (1861-1938), Norwegian Arctic explorer, scientist, statesman, and humanitarian. During the period that Hemingway was writing this story, Nansen was high commissioner of refugees for the League of Nations.

- **weinstube** German for a tavern that specializes in various wines.

- **skischule** German for a skiing school.

- **sans voir** French for the concept of "not seeing."

- **Kaiser Jagers** Alpine troops.

- **Vorarlberg, Arlberg** winter resorts in the Austrian Tirol country.

- **Kirsch** a cherry-flavored liquor.

- **Crillon** a well-known Paris hotel, used frequently in Hemingway's works.

- **Memsahib** a Hindustani word meaning "lady."

- **jodpurs** A type of trousers, named after the Indian state of Jodhpur, they end right below the knee and flare around the hips.

- **Klim** trade name for a kind of powdered milk (spell it backward).

- **mosquito boots** loose boots into which trousers are tucked.

- **boric** boric acid, a mild disinfectant.

- **Constantinople**   the former name for what is now Istanbul.

- **Bosphorus**   the strait that separates Asia from Europe, made famous by Romantic poets who would try to swim across.

- **Anatolia**   the great plains area of Turkey.

- **Constantine officers**   At the time, these royal officers bore the name of the king of Greece, King Constantine.

- **ballet skirts**   During the time that Hemingway wrote the story, Greek troops in the mountains wore uniforms exactly like Hemingway describes.

- **saucers**   In various cities in Europe, drinks are served on saucers; when refills are ordered, saucers are placed atop one another; when one pays the bill, the waiter counts the number of saucers.

- *Spur* **and** *Town and Country*   Two "high society" magazines.

- **Schwarzwald**   The Black Forest of Bavaria, in the southern part of Germany.

- **inflation**   Germany suffered a terrible inflation in the middle 1920s and was eventually helped economically to recover by the United States and its so-called Dodge Plan.

- **marc**   a kind of brandy.

- **bal musette**   a public dance hall.

- **concierge**   the manager of an apartment house in Europe.

- **Garde Republicaine**   resplendently uniformed troops that guarded the French Parliament.

- **locataire**   a tenant.

- *L'Auto*   a Paris newspaper devoted to sports news.

- **sportifs**   the sporting kind.

- **Communards**   After the French defeat in the Franco-Prussian War (1871), a communal government, in opposition to the national one, was set up in Paris. There followed a brief civil war; afterward, 17,000 Parisian followers of the Communards were executed, including women and children. Hemingway is referring to the descendants of these people.

- **boucherie chevaline**   a horse butcher; in many parts of Europe, horse meat is eaten quite commonly.

- **Paul Verlaine**   French poet (1844-96); considered one of the greatest poets of the nineteenth century.

- **ivresse** drunkenness.

- **femme de ménage** a housekeeper.

- **stick bomb** German hand grenades had handles; during World War II, the Allies often referred to them as "potato mashers."

- **lorry** British for truck.

- **wildebeeste** Dutch for wild beast, a form of gnu or antelope that is found in Africa.

- **daughter's debut** a monied coming-out party for a young lady, to formally introduce her to high society.

- **Nairobi** the capital of Kenya.

- **Kilimanjaro** the highest peak in Africa, approximately 19,317 feet.

CHARACTER ANALYSES

NICK ADAMS

Nick Adams is the name that Hemingway gave to the fictional persona, largely autobiographical, whom he often wrote about. Like Hemingway himself, Nick is the son of a doctor ("The Indian Camp"; "The Doctor and the Doctor's Wife"); he relishes fishing and hunting in the northern peninsula of Michigan ("Big Two-Hearted River"). He romances a young girl named Marjorie, a summer waitress at a summer resort ("The End of Something"; "The Three-Day Blow"). He goes abroad during World War I and serves as an American Red Cross ambulance driver; he also is a courier, carrying chocolates and cigarettes to Italian soldiers on the Austro-Italian battlefront. And, like Hemingway, Nick suffers a knee wound ("In Another Country"). Unlike Hemingway, however, Nick suffered post-traumatic shock; his mind periodically seems to come unhinged ("A Way You'll Never Be").

In all, Hemingway wrote at least a dozen stories that center around Nick Adams, and in 1972, Scribner's published a volume entitled *The Nick Adams Stories*.

In each of the Nick Adams stories, Nick witnesses—or is a part of—some traumatic event, and Hemingway reveals Nick's reaction to that event. For example, in "Indian Camp," Hemingway focuses on Nick's reaction to a young American Indian man's slitting his throat from ear to ear after listening to his young wife scream for two days and then scream even more during Dr. Adams' cesarean that delivers a baby boy. In "The Doctor and the Doctor's Wife," Nick's blind hero-worship of his father is contrasted with our knowledge that Nick's father has a fraudulent aspect to his character. "The End of Something" and "The Three-Day Blow" revolve around Nick's breaking off with his girlfriend, Marjorie. Nick is not entirely happy with himself afterward; Nick's friend Bill prodded him to break up with her, and, finally, Nick secretly rejoices that he need not be as thoroughly against marriage as Bill is: Romance and women can still be tantalizing; they need not be shackles on a man's future success.

Nick's stay in Summit, Illinois, in "The Killers" ends when he is forced to witness a former prizefighter calmly await certain death by two hired killers. When Nick was a boy, he vowed never to be afraid of death, never to be like the young American Indian husband who "couldn't stand" life's demands. Yet here, Nick leaves Summit. He can't stand to remain in a town where a man lacks the courage to do battle with death—even certain death.

"Big Two-Hearted River" follows Nick after he returns to Michigan from the Italian front during World War I. He takes a train to the upper peninsula and hikes to a stream where he will camp and fish and be alone, where he will slowly perform the rote motions of self-sustaining chores, peeling away the trauma and the scars from his ragged, wounded spirit and newly empowering himself with the healing powers of nature's rituals.

FRANCIS MACOMBER

Macomber is thirty-five years old, very tall and well built, at the apex of his manhood—fit and good at court games (by "court games," Hemingway is referring to tennis or squash, games in which there are rules and perimeters for the game). Now, however, the very wealthy and very handsome Macomber has come on safari to hunt wild game. This is no court game. There are no perimeters here—and few rules. The jungle is endless, and the law is the law of the jungle—or the law of the survivor, the fittest.

When the story opens, Macomber has returned from a lion hunt. He is hailed as a hero, but we discover that when confronted with the lion, he ran. Macomber's wife saw him become a distraught coward. Wilson, their British guide, witnessed the event. Macomber has to reclaim a sense of manhood for himself and regain their admiration. He has his chance when he is face-to-face with a charging water buffalo. His courage is magnificent—and then he is shot, at the very moment when he feels happier than he's felt in years. His short, happy life flares up, then dies, quickly.

MARGOT MACOMBER

Macomber's beautiful wife, whom he married because of her beauty, secretly despises Macomber because she knows that he married her for one reason only: She is his "trophy wife." She despises herself because she knows that she married him for one reason only: He is very rich. He will never divorce her because he values her beauty; she will never divorce him because she has become comfortable with being a very rich wife.

Therefore, Margot is delighted when Macomber proves to be such a weakling and runs from the lion; it gives her psychological control over him. It's something that she can goad him with. However, when Macomber is about to reclaim his manhood as he faces the water buffalo, she is so frightened of losing control over him that she fires (or perhaps pretends to fire) at the charging water buffalo—and, instead, shoots her husband.

HARRY

Hemingway does not tell us Harry's last name; we know only that he is a writer and that he and his wife, Helen, are on a safari in East Africa. Their truck has malfunctioned, and, while trying to fix it, Harry scratched himself and neglected applying iodine to the scratch. Now, gangrene has begun to eat away at the flesh on his right leg. The stench is overpowering. However, he's not in pain—physical pain. All of his pain seems to be emotional pain of the seemingly sure knowledge that he is dying—and, worse than dying, he's dying without having written many stories that he'd planned to write.

Why didn't he write these stories? Harry believes that it was probably because he married a woman with a fortune. Her money poisoned his writing future, just as surely as gangrene is now poisoning his body and gnawing away at the few days of life that he has left.

When Harry is not being sarcastically savage to Helen, he drifts in and out of interior monologue flashbacks, remembering and recalling people and geography and incidents that he's kept in his scrapbook of memories. They will die with him. No one will ever write about them now.

HELEN

Harry's wife seems almost saint-like, especially when compared with her dying husband. She does everything she can to make his illness more comfortable. She is genuinely concerned with his failing strength and tries to give him hope and courage.

CRITICAL ESSAY

HEMINGWAY'S STYLE

A great deal has been written about Hemingway's distinctive style. In fact, the two great stylists of twentieth-century American literature are William Faulkner and Ernest Hemingway, and the styles of the two writers are so vastly different that there can be no comparison. For example, their styles have become so famous and so individually unique that yearly contests award prizes to people who write the best parodies of their styles. The parodies of Hemingway's writing style are perhaps the more fun to read because of Hemingway's ultimate simplicity and because he so often used the same style and the same themes in much of his work.

From the beginning of his writing career in the 1920s, Hemingway's writing style occasioned a great deal of comment and controversy. Basically, a typical Hemingway novel or short story is written in simple, direct, unadorned prose. Possibly, the style developed because of his early journalistic training. The reality, however, is this: Before Hemingway began publishing his short stories and sketches, American writers affected British mannerisms. Adjectives piled on top of one another; adverbs tripped over each other. Colons clogged the flow of even short paragraphs, and the plethora of semicolons often caused readers to throw up their hands in exasperation. And then came Hemingway.

An excellent example of Hemingway's style is found in "A Clean, Well-Lighted Place." In this story, there is no maudlin sentimentality; the plot is simple, yet highly complex and difficult. Focusing on an old man and two waiters, Hemingway says as little as possible. He lets the characters speak, and, from them, we discover the inner loneliness of two of the men and the callous prejudices of the other. When Hemingway was awarded the Nobel Prize in literature in 1954, his writing style was singled out as one of his foremost achievements. The committee recognized his "forceful and style-making mastery of the art of modern narration."

Hemingway has often been described as a master of dialogue; in story after story, novel after novel, readers and critics have remarked, "This is the way that these characters would really talk." Yet, a close examination of his dialogue reveals that this is *rarely* the way people really speak. The effect is accomplished, rather, by calculated emphasis and repetition that makes us remember what has been said.

Perhaps some of the best of Hemingway's much-celebrated use of dialogue occurs in "Hills Like White Elephants." When the story opens, two characters—a man and a woman—are sitting at a table. We finally learn that the girl's nickname is "Jig." Eventually we learn that they are in the cafe of a train station in Spain. But Hemingway tells us nothing about them—or about their past or about their future. There is no description of them. We don't know their ages. We know virtually nothing about them. The only information that we have about them is what we learn from their dialogue; thus this story must be read very carefully.

This spare, carefully honed and polished writing style of Hemingway was by no means spontaneous. When he worked as a journalist, he learned to report facts crisply and succinctly. He was also an obsessive revisionist. It is reported that he wrote and rewrote all, or portions, of *The Old Man and the Sea* more than two hundred times before he was ready to release it for publication.

Hemingway took great pains with his work; he revised tirelessly. "A writer's style," he said, "should be direct and personal, his imagery rich and earthy, and his words simple and vigorous." Hemingway more than fulfilled his own requirements for good writing. His words are simple and vigorous, burnished and uniquely brilliant.

REVIEW QUESTIONS AND ESSAY TOPICS

(1) In "Indian Camp," what is the effect of the young husband's death on Nick Adams?

(2) How does Dr. Adams, in "Indian Camp," explain suicide to Nick? What does he say about men who commit suicide and women who commit suicide?

(3) In "The Doctor and the Doctor's Wife," why is Dr. Adams angry at Dick Boulton's sarcasm about the logs that he is about to cut up for firewood?

(4) Describe the tense relationship between Dr. Adams and his wife in "The Doctor and the Doctor's Wife."

(5) In "The End of Something," what excuse does Nick give Marjorie for breaking off their relationship? What prompts Nick to dissolve the relationship?

(6) What role does Bill play, in relation to Nick, in "The End of Something" and "The Three–Day Blow"?

(7) Why is the title "The Three-Day Blow" apropos to the plot of this story?

(8) Describe Al and Max in "The Killers."

(9) How are Andreson and the young Indian husband (in "Indian Camp") similar?

(10) How do Hemingway's style and Nick Adams' "craziness" in "A Way You'll Never Be" parallel each other?

(11) How was Nick injured in "A Way You'll Never Be"?

(12) Contrast the major and the hunting hawks in "In Another Country."

(13) Besides the loss of the use of his fencing hand, what other loss does the major suffer in "In Another Country"?

(14) What is the setting of "Big Two-Hearted River"? Why do you suppose Hemingway chose this particular setting?

(15) In "The Short Happy Life," how is Macomber's first safari, his conquest of wild animals, different from all of his previous victories?

(16) Why did Macomber marry Margot? Why does he stay married to her?

(17) Why does Margot resent Macomber?

(18) In "Hills Like White Elephants," who likens the hills to white elephants? For what purpose?

(19) How does the man describe the operation that he hopes that the girl will agree to? What is her attitude toward the medical procedure?

(20) In "A Clean, Well-Lighted Place," why is this descriptive title a key to the meaning of the story?

(21) What do the older waiter and the old man have in common?

(22) In "The Snows of Kilimanjaro," what is Harry's profession? Is he a success in his profession?

(23) What is Helen's attitude toward her husband?

(24) Describe the plane ride toward the square top of Kilimanjaro.

SELECTED BIBLIOGRAPHY

_____. *Hemingway: The Writer as Artist*. Princeton, NJ: Princeton University Press, 1973.

BASS, EBEN. "Hemingway's Women of *In Another Country*." *Markham Review* 6 (1977): 35-39.

BENSON, JACKSON J. New Critical Approaches to the Short Stories of Ernest Hemingway. Durham, NC: Duke University Press, 1990.

BRENNER, GERRY. *Concealments in Hemingway's Works*. Columbus: Ohio State University Press, 1983.

BURGESS, ANTHONY. *Ernest Hemingway and His World*. London: Thames and Hudson, 1978.

COX, JAMES M. "Getting the Best of Ernest." *Sewanee Review* 96.3 (1988): 511-15.

DONALDSON, SCOTT. *By Force of Will: The Life and Art of Ernest Hemingway*. New York: The Viking Press, 1977.

FLORA, JOSEPH M. *Ernest Hemingway: A Study of the Short Fiction*. Boston: Twain Publishers, 1989.

GRIFFIN, PETER. *Along with Youth: Hemingway, the Early Years*. Oxford: Oxford University Press, 1985.

HAYS, PETER. "Hemingway, Faulkner, and a Bicycle Built for Death." *Notes on Modern American Literature*. 5.4 (1981): N.pag.

HEMINGWAY, JACK. *Misadventures of a Fly Fisherman: My Life With and without Papa*. Dallas: Taylor Publishing Company, 1986.

JOOST, NICHOLAS. *Ernest Hemingway and the Little Magazines: The Paris Years*. Barre, MA: Barre Publishers, 1968.

JOSEPHS, ALLEN. "In Another Country: Hemingway and Spain." *North Dakota Quarterly* 60.2 (1992): 50-57.

LARSON, KELLI A. *Ernest Hemingway: A Reference Guide, 1974-1989.* Boston: G.K. Hall, 1991.

MANDEL, MIRIAM B. *Reading Hemingway: The Facts in the Fictions.* Metuchen, NJ: The Scarecrow Press, 1995.

MONTGOMERY, CONSTANCE CAPPEL. *Hemingway in Michigan.* New York: Fleet Publishing Corporation, 1966.

OHLE, WILLIAM H. *How It Was in Horton Bay.* Horton Bay, Boyne City, MI: Ohle Publications, 1989.

REYNOLDS, MICHAEL. *The Young Hemingway.* Oxford: Basil Blackwell, 1986.

ROBINSON, FORREST. "Hemingway's Invisible Hero of *In Another Country.*" *Essays in Literature* 15.2 (1988): 237-44.

SANGWAN, SURENDER SINGH, and STYAPAL DAHIYA. "Money and Morals in Hemingway's Short Stories." *Panjab University Research Bulletin* 21.2 (1990): 69.73.

SMITH, PAUL. *A Reader's Guide to the Short Stories of Ernest Hemingway.* Boston: G.K. Hall, 1989.

SOENS, A. L. "Hemingway and Hawks: The Hierarchy of Heroism in *In Another Country.*" *English Language Notes* 28.2 (1990): 62.79.

STEINKE, JAMES. "Hemingway's 'In Another Country' and 'Now I Lay Me.'" *The Hemingway Review* 5.1 (1985): 32-39.

WAGNER, LINDA W., ed. *Ernest Hemingway: Six Decades of Criticism.* Lansing: Michigan State University Press, 1987.

WILLIAMS, WIRT. *The Tragic Art of Ernest Hemingway.* Baton Rouge: Louisiana State University Press, 1981.

INTERNET SOURCES

http://members.aol.com/rshaw10353/mich/
http://members.atlantic.net/ ~ gagne/hem/shorts.html
http://vccslitonline.cc.va.us/copy_of_hills
http://www.bridgewater.edu/ ~ sgallowa/450/hemingway/iot.htm
http://www.upnorth.net/hemi